FACETS OF THE RENAISSANCE

Edited by WILLIAM H. WERKMEISTER, PH.D., *Director of the School of Philosophy and Professor of Philosophy in the University of Southern California*

Foreword by TRACY E. STREVEY, PH.D., LL.D., *Dean of the College of Letters, Arts, and Sciences and Professor of History in the University of Southern California*

FACETS OF THE RENAISSANCE

Essays by WALLACE K. FERGUSON

GARRETT MATTINGLY · E. HARRIS HARBISON

MYRON P. GILMORE · PAUL OSKAR KRISTELLER

HARPER TORCHBOOKS   THE ACADEMY LIBRARY

Harper & Row, Publishers   New York, Evanston, and London

HARPER TORCHBOOKS / *The Academy Library*

Advisory Editor in the Humanities and Social Sciences: Benjamin Nelson

Foreword

HIS VOLUME PRESENTS A SELECTED GROUP OF FIVE essays, chosen from the "Arensberg Lectures" on the Renaissance which were given by a group of distinguished scholars invited to the campus of the University of Southern California during the spring of 1956. Generous financial support provided by the Francis Bacon Foundation made possible the original lectures, as well as the publication of this book. Since the Foundation was established through the interest of Walter C. and Louise Stevens Arensberg, it was fitting that the name "Arensberg Lectures" be used to designate the series. The University is indeed grateful for the assistance of the Foundation and, in particular, expresses its appreciation to Mrs. Elizabeth Wrigley, President of the Francis Bacon Foundation.

The Renaissance scholars participating in the program were Wallace K. Ferguson, New York University, now associated with the University of West Ontario; Garrett Mattingly, Columbia; E. Harris Harbison, Princeton; Myron P. Gilmore, Harvard; Paul O. Kristeller, Columbia. Each participant gave three lectures, open to the public, and consulted with various seminar groups and students on campus.

In these days of rapid and violent change involving new dimensions for the human race, it is easy to become concerned only with the contemporary manifestations of a new accelerating technology. It is good to realize that despite modern emphasis upon the present, there are those—scholars and teachers, students and peoples of many lands—who are also concerned with the values and great cultural traditions which have marked the evolution of man and civilization.

The University of Southern California is proud to present this significant volume, which by no means attempts to cover all phases of the Renaissance but which does bring scholarly interpretation and enlightenment to a period of human history important then and now. To some the Renaissance has meant specific achievements in the arts and sciences and in religious, economic, and political developments. To others its significance lies in the advancement of philosophical thought, the evolution of ideas, and impact on learning. Probably no one interpretation is valid alone; only through a synthesis of many aspects can a proper perspective be achieved. It is hoped that this volume contributes to a broadened and orderly understanding of a most complex period.

TRACY E. STREVEY, *Dean*
College of Letters, Arts, and Sciences
University of Southern California

Table of Contents

WALLACE K. FERGUSON ∿ *The Reinterpretation of the Renaissance*

ISTORIANS OF EVERY GENERATION SINCE PETRARCH
have contributed to the interpretation or rein-
terpretation of the Renaissance; but it is only
in the past half century that it has become an
acutely controversial problem in historiography.[1] Bit by bit, generations of humanists,
Protestant historians, rationalists, and romantics built up the conception of the revival of art, letters, and learning, until in the
mid-nineteenth century Jacob Burckhardt fused the traditional
views, with some very significant additions of his own, into a
synthetic picture of the Renaissance as a distinct period in the
cultural history of western Europe. The historians who followed
in Burckhardt's footsteps must have been very happy men. They
knew what the Renaissance was. This period of idyllic certainty,
however, was not left long undisturbed. Criticism of the master's
conception began even before the end of the nineteenth century,
though it was generally ignored. Since that time revisionists in
increasing numbers and working from a variety of directions have
collaborated in the task of bringing chaos out of order. And so
far as can be discerned at the moment, the end is not yet.

No Renaissance historian today can be unaware of the conflict of
interpretations. Most of the historians in this country, whose spe-

cialty lies in other fields, however, have tended, at least until very recently, to take the various interpretations of the Renaissance more or less for granted, and have been unconsciously rather than consciously influenced by them. Busy with their own specific tasks, they have not taken the time to study the varying trends of Renaissance historiography nor, perhaps, to consider very definitely their own stand in relation to them. In this country we have been rather wary of definite historical interpretations and philosophies of history. And perhaps rightly so. But however much we may shy away from the *Begriff*-stricken Teutonic tendency toward the abstract conception and the *ismus*, we cannot write or teach history without giving it some interpretation, and it may be as well that that interpretation should be a conscious one and that we should be aware of its relation to the historical writing of the past and present. The following brief sketch of the main currents in the history of Renaissance historiography, concluding somewhat rashly with the approach to the interpretation of the Renaissance which I myself have found most satisfactory, is directed primarily to scholars who are not specialists in Renaissance history and is proffered in the hope that it may provoke some thought and discussion, even if it does not, God save the mark, help to clarify the issue.

Looking back over the long evolution of the idea of the Renaissance and its more recent vicissitudes, I am impressed by the fact that the relation of the Renaissance to the Middle Ages is the crucial point. Its relation to modern civilization is a subsidiary problem, dependent on the historian's notion of the extent to which Renaissance culture differed from that of the Middle Ages and the directions in which the deviation occurred. For centuries the conceptions of the Renaissance were shaped by men who disliked what they knew of medieval culture, and the more recent revisions of the traditional interpretation have come, for the most part, from men who for one reason or another felt drawn to some aspect of medieval civilization. In either case Renaissance historiography has fairly bristled with value judgments.

The Italian humanists, who laid the first foundations for the modern periodization of history, as well as for the conception of a rebirth of art and letters after the Middle Ages, were certainly guilty enough in this respect. Their admiration for classical culture led them to draw a clear line of demarcation between antiquity and the period of barbaric darkness that followed the decline of the Roman Empire. Petrarch thought ancient history ended when the emperors became Christian.[2] Flavio Biondo set the date somewhat later and more definitely at the year 410.[3] The humanists thus set up one of the boundaries of the Middle Ages; but their view of the thousand years that were later given that name varied, depending on the aspect of history which occupied them at the moment. As the political historians of the Italian states, they treated the whole period from the first appearance of the communes as one of steady growth down to their own day.[4] But as classical scholars, the products of an urban and secular society, they found much less to value in the culture of the period between the decline of ancient civilization and the recent revival of art and classical learning in Italy. Almost without exception they ignored the whole body of medieval feudal and ecclesiastical literature and leaped straight from the decline of ancient culture to the age of Giotto and Dante or, more commonly, Petrarch. Between those two ages art and letters were dead, neglected, buried, sleeping, prostrate in the dust—these phrases occur over and over again—until they were revived or restored to the light by the great Italian masters of the fourteenth and fifteenth centuries. For this revival the humanists as a rule suggested no cause except the unexplained phenomenon of individual genius; though Leonardo Bruni, the Florentine historian, found a causal relation in the recovery of freedom by the Italian cities.[5] The Italian humanists, in their capacity as historians, contributed only these ingredients to the full conception of the Renaissance: that art and letters were dead for a period of centuries; that the revival coincided with the restoration of classical literature; and that it was the work of the genius of the Italian masters. But these ideas were to live for centuries among men whose tastes were formed by the classical traditions of education.

Where the Italian humanists had been generally content to pass over medieval culture as though it were nonexistent, the Erasmian humanists of the North added a positive factor to the conception of medieval darkness by a vitriolic attack upon scholasticism. Erasmus was convinced that both religion and learning had declined sadly since the time of the last classical writers and the Fathers of the Church, and that a reform could come only through a return to the sources in their ancient purity. The medieval system of education, he thought, was largely responsible for the *de*formation of both Christianity and good letters and in his own day it was still the principal barrier to reform.[6]

After the Reformation, the Protestant historians seized eagerly upon the conception of medieval culture thus developed by the humanists and used it as a propagandist weapon against the Roman church. For two centuries and more, Protestant interpretations of medieval history were oriented by the necessity of proving that the light of the Gospel had been progressively obscured by the malign influence of the popes and their scholastic agents, with the result that Western Christendom had remained for a thousand years sunk in barbaric ignorance, superstition, and spiritual sloth. Philipp Melanchthon described medieval learning as a barbaric mixture of two evils: ignorant yet garrulous philosophy and the cult of idols.[7] And Bishop John Bale, popularly known as "bilious" Bale because of his talent for invective, in one of his milder moments concluded that the mere description of this sordid, obscure, and ignoble kind of writing was enough to move generous and well-born minds to nausea.[8]

For the Protestant historians the Reformation was the beginning of a new age in the history of the church, but they also hailed the revival of learning as marking the dawn of the new day. Viewed from this angle the renaissance of letters became a movement inspired by Divine Providence to prepare the way for the acceptance of the Gospel. The genius of the Italian masters dropped into the background as the theologians sought some more evident sign of God's handiwork. John Foxe, the author of the *Book of Martyrs*, found the origins of the movement in that "admirable work of God's Wisdom," the invention of printing, through which by God's grace "good wits" were stirred up "aptly to conceive the light of knowledge and judgment, by which light darkness began to be espied and ignorance to be detected, truth from error, religion from superstition to be discerned."[9] Théodore de Bèze, on the other hand, ascribed the revival to the fall of Constantinople and the flight of the Greek refugees to Italy.[10]

This latter idea took firm root in the following centuries among Northern historians who were but slightly interested in the earlier history of the Italian revival and to whom the cataclysmic cause appealed with all the charm of a theory that made further thought unnecessary. Thanks to Vasari, whose *Lives of the Great Painters, Sculptors and Architects*[11] had made the *rinascità dell' arte* in the age of Giotto and his contemporaries a standard conception, the early history of the revival of art was never forgotten; but through the seventeenth and eighteenth centuries the revival of learning was generally regarded as beginning in the age of the Medici. Meanwhile, the periodization of history implicit in the humanist pattern of cultural history and in the Protestant scheme of church history was reinforced by a growing appreciation of the significance of the explorations and discoveries and of the rise of the national states around 1500. Before the end of the seventeenth century it had hardened into the formal divisions of ancient, medieval, and modern history which still dominate our historical thought. In this scheme of periodization, the Renaissance, in its limited identification with the revival of learning and art, became merely one of the phenomena that marked the beginning of the modern age.

It was thus that the eighteenth century historians treated it, but they gave the revival of learning a new interpretation and a new significance. For them it was the first stage in the modern progress of reason. David Hume regarded it as one of the symptoms of what he called "the dawn of civility and science."[12] Like the Protestant historians, if for different reasons, the historians of the Enlightenment condemned both the religion and the learning of the Middle Ages as ignorant, superstitious, and barbarous. Like the humanists, too, they judged the literature and art of the past by classical standards, though their classicism was more rigid than that of the humanists and they added to the condemnation of medieval culture a more positive revulsion against its irrationality, eccentricity, and general formlessness. For the eighteenth century, then, the revival of art and learning under classical influences meant both the restoration of good taste and the liberation of human reason. Edward Gibbon summed up this classical-rationalist interpretation of the literary revival with the ponderous authority that only he could achieve:

Before the revival of classic literature, the barbarians in Europe were immersed in ignorance; and their vulgar tongues were marked with the rudeness and poverty of their manners. The students of the more perfect idioms of Rome and Greece were introduced to a new world of light and science; to the society of the free and polished nations of antiquity; and to a familiar intercourse with the immortal men who spoke the sublime language of eloquence and reason. . . . As soon as it had been deeply saturated with the celestial dews, the soil was quickened into vegetation and life; the modern idioms were refined; the classics of Athens and Rome inspired a pure taste and a generous emulation; and in Italy, as afterwards in France and England, the pleasing reign of poetry and fiction was succeeded by the light of speculative and experimental philosophy.[13]

But if Gibbon placed the greater emphasis on the influence of the classics, Voltaire laid greater stress on intellectual progress, and on the spontaneous development of Italian genius. He described the history of Western Europe as "l'histoire de l'extinction, de la renaissance, et du progrès de l'esprit humain."[14] And of all the European peoples the Italians were the first to emerge from the grossièreté of the Middle Ages. In the fourteenth and fifteenth centuries, "barbarism, superstition, and ignorance covered the face of the earth, except in Italy."[15] The Italians had a monopoly of genius. They were the most intelligent people in the world, and only in their rich cities could men live with comfort and enjoy the good things of life. Voltaire gave full value to the independent rebirth of the vernacular literature and the fine arts in the fourteenth century, but described the age of the Medici, which followed the fall of Constantinople and the revival of learning, as one of the four ages in human history that might be counted happy by a man of thought and taste. Voltaire's picture of Renaissance society, however, was not without its dark side. He was the first to stress the moral confusion, the irreligious attitude, and the criminal tendencies which were to become the distinguishing characteristics of the Italian Renaissance in nineteenth century historiography. Apparently assuming that such would be the natural result of the growth of learning and reason, Voltaire concluded that the leading classes in Italy had rejected Christianity. But true philosophy and natural religion, the products of the age of reason, had not yet been discovered. Hence the moral chaos of the Renaissance. "No century," he declared, "was so prolific in assassinations, poisonings, treasons, and monstrous debauches."[16]

The tradition of medieval darkness and of the rebirth of art, letters, and reason lasted into the nineteenth century. It was re-echoed by Roscoe, Hallam, and Michelet. True, it was no longer undisputed. The Romantic Movement introduced a rehabilitation of the Middle Ages. In reaction against rationalist values, the romantic historians idealized the chivalry, the religious aspirations, the poetry, and art forms of feudal and monastic society. Yet this reversal of values did nothing to minimize the contrast between medieval and Renaissance culture. If anything, the romantic historians heightened the contrast, added color to the rational wickedness of the Renaissance, and regarded the age of the Medici and the Borgias with a kind of fascinated horror.

Thus far the conception of the Renaissance *per se* had been limited to the revival of learning or the *renaissance des lettres et des beaux arts*. Nearly all the ingredients of what became the traditional conception of the Renaissance were already present, but they had not yet been fused together into a comprehensive synthesis, extended to include the whole civilization of the period. The Hegelian philosophy of history, with its emphasis on the creative action of the Idea, on the *Volksgeist* and the *Zeitgeist*, pointed the way toward a periodic conception of the Renaissance as a "moment in the life of the spirit," and Michelet had used the term "Renaissance" in a periodic sense.[17] But it was not till the publication of Jacob Burckhardt's *Civilization of the Renaissance in Italy*[18] that the Renaissance was finally established as a separate period in *Kulturgeschichte*.

Burckhardt's Renaissance marked the culmination of the long tradition of medieval darkness and the rebirth of culture. In it the classical and rationalist strains of interpretation were particularly strong, but the whole synthesis would have been impossible before the nineteenth century, and some of its most characteristic features were a direct reflection of Burckhardt's own personality. Burckhardt combined historical insight and a rare capacity for synthesis with the mental and emotional bias of the aesthete and the intellectual aristocrat. Hence his peculiar emphasis on the conscious artistry of Renaissance institutions and on the liberation of individual personality from the corporate bondage of the Middle Ages. His interpretation appealed strongly to the aestheticism and liberalism as well as to the Hegelian idealism of the later nineteenth century. It carried conviction by the consummate artistry with which every aspect of Renaissance life was fitted into its place in an integrated whole, and the perfection of the synthesis helped to conceal the fact that it was a static picture.

But there is little need to dwell upon the Burckhardtian conception of the Renaissance. It is familiar enough. For half a century Renaissance historians did little more than repeat and amplify it, extending it to the Northern countries and appropriating to the Renaissance every indication of new life that they discovered in the Middle Ages. Even when historians began to depart from it in one direction or another, it remained the norm by which the deviations were measured.

The revisions of Burckhardt's formula, which have become increasingly numerous in the past four or five decades, proceeded from a variety of sources; from the religious romanticism of the late nineteenth century, which carried over into the Thomist revival of more recent Catholicism; from the growing nationalism, which in Germany was identified with a Pan-Germanic racial doctrine and in France with a belligerent assertion of French national culture; from a great increase in both the quantity and intensity of medieval studies, which coincided with a general decline in classical education, particularly in this country; and, closely associated with this, the extension of historical research to economic and social fields. Perhaps I might add, too, the natural tendency of historians, most of whom are professors, to think otherwise.

From these and other sources has come an increasing criticism of the following characteristics of the Burckhardtian Renaissance: the causative and determining influence of the revival of classical antiquity; the exclusively Italian origins of Renaissance thought; the unique individualism of Renaissance society; and, finally, the whole conception of the Renaissance as a separate period with a coherent and unchanging character, sharply contrasted with the Middle Ages.

The first notable departure from the classical-rational aspects of Burckhardt's interpretation appeared in the religious romanticism of Henry Thode's *Franz von Assisi und die Anfänge der Kunst der Renaissance in Italien*, first published in 1885. It was Thode's thesis that the individualism of the Renaissance, its subjective energy, and its reconciliation of religion with nature were the results not of the revival of antiquity, but of the religious mysticism and subjectivism of the Middle Ages. The figure of the saint of Assisi occupied the center of his picture. He was represented as both the culmination of one great trend in medieval religion and the inspiration of the Italian culture of the following two centuries, out of which, in turn, grew both humanism and the Reformation. Thode's book made little stir among the historians until his conception of St. Francis was reinforced by Paul Sabatier's unforgettable biography.[19] Since then, however, there has been a growing appreciation of the Christian content in Renaissance thought at the expense of the classical and rational. Émile Gebhardt and Konrad Burdach were directly influenced by Thode, and one might also mention among those who have stressed the continuity of Christian tradition in Italian humanism H. O. Taylor, Alfred von Martin, Ernst Walser, Giuseppe Toffanin, and, more recently, Douglas Bush.[20] It was not so necessary to demonstrate the Christian quality of Northern humanism, though Augustin Renaudet[21] and others have done so at great length. The relation between humanism and late medieval mysticism in the North has been pointed out by Paul Mestwerdt and Albert Hyma.[22]

The classical element in Renaissance culture has also suffered from the attacks of the national and racial schools of Northern historians. Early in this century Carl Neumann attempted to prove by the example of Byzantium that classical antiquity could not stimulate a new intellectual life, and asserted the revolutionary thesis that the vigor of Renaissance culture was a natural flowering of the one vital force in medieval civilization, namely *Deutsches Barbarentum*.[23] Since then the Germanic thesis has been carried to the extreme of claiming direct Lombard or Gothic descent for all the geniuses of the Italian Renaissance from Dante to Michelangelo. More commonly, however, the recent German historians have been willing to admit the Italian national character of the Renaissance in Italy, but have insisted on the spontaneous and independent development of German culture. In much the same way, the French art historian Louis Courajod and the Fleming Fierens Gevaert proclaimed not only the independent development of French and Burgundian art but also its priority to the Italian, thus reversing the stream of influence across the Alps.[24] In the field of literature and learning, too, recent French historians have been at pains to demonstrate the continuity of development from medieval France through the Renaissance. In doing so they have tended either to minimize the influence of the classics

and stress that of the medieval French vernacular literature or to
claim the revival of antiquity for the twelfth and thirteenth centuries when France still held the cultural hegemony of western
Europe.

The rehabilitation of medieval culture, however, owes most to
the scholarly work of recent medievalists who cannot be accused
either of undue romanticism or of national or racial bias; and it
is from them that has come the most serious attack upon the conception of the Renaissance as a sudden, dazzling revival of classical learning, rational thought, and free individualism. Elsewhere
I have called this movement "The Revolt of the Medievalists."[25]
Charles Homer Haskins, Franz von Bezold, and others demonstrated the extent of the classical revival of the twelfth century.[26]
H. O. Taylor insisted on the continuity of both the classical and
the Christian traditions.[27] Helen Waddell in her charming book
on the wandering scholars has demonstrated a feeling for the
beauties of nature and the joys of this world among medieval
poets influenced by classical models.[28] Étienne Gilson, the cham-
pion of scholastic philosophy, carried his defence of medieval
thought still further and asserted the absolute superiority of the
schoolmen over the humanists in both the recovery of antiquity
and rational thought, and Jacques Maritain has called Scholasticism the true humanism.[29] Lynn Thorndyke and George Sarton
have asserted a somewhat similar thesis in relation to science,
tending to see in humanism a decline of systematic ratiocination
for which the aesthetic interests of the humanists were an insuffi-
cient compensation;[30] and James Westfall Thompson has discovered a more extensive lay education in the Middle Ages than
had generally been supposed.[31] Art historians, too, have contributed, perhaps more than their share, to the reversal of value
judgments about medieval and Renaissance culture. Finally, in a
book by no means free from special pleading, the francophile
Swedish historian, Johan Nordström, has translated all the characteristics of the Burckhardtian Renaissance back into the twelfth
and thirteenth centuries.[32] This tendency to discover the Ren-

aissance in the Middle Ages has also been accompanied by a parallel tendency to find much of the Middle Ages in the Renaissance and to view the latter period, in Huizinga's phrase, as the "waning of the Middle Ages"[33] rather than as what Hume called "the dawn of civility and science."

One major result of all this has been a new emphasis on the continuity of historical development. Burckhardt's Italian Renaissance has thus been deprived of the unique character which differentiated it so clearly from the preceding period and from the contemporary culture of the northern countries. It has also been deprived of much of its internal integration by the substitution of a dynamic conception for a relatively static portrayal of the spirit of the age.

The recognition of historical continuity is always, I think, a healthy tendency, and one that was particularly necessary in the interpretation of the Renaissance because of the deeply rooted tradition of its complete differentiation from and superiority over everything medieval. But, granting the corrective value of the recent tendency, is it not possible that the historians who are influenced by it are in danger of discrediting unduly much that was worth while in Burckhardt's conception and, above all, of losing sight of the very real differences between the prevailing tone of Renaissance civilization and that of the twelfth and thirteenth centuries? To carry the criticism of Burckhardt's Renaissance to the point of abandoning the Renaissance as a period altogether is, I think, unnecessary and deplorable. The term "Renaissance" itself may be open to objection. It has unfortunate connections. But there is as yet no other recognized term for a period which, I think, requires recognition.

I have been happy to note in the last decade or so a swing of the pendulum back toward appreciation of the originality of Renaissance culture. Some extremely important contributions to this tendency have been made by the historians of music, notably, Heinrich Besseler, Gustave Reese, Albert Einstein, and Edward Lowinsky.[34] The history of music in the Middle Ages and the

Renaissance has been until recently a much neglected field, but one capable of furnishing valuable illustrations of the changes in cultural tone through these two ages. Among art historians, Erwin Panofsky[35] has done much to rehabilitate the concept of the Renaissance, as Ernst Cassirer and P. O. Kristeller have done for the history of philosophy[36] and Garrett Mattingly for that of diplomacy.[37]

It should be understood, of course, that recognition of the Renaissance as a period in history does not imply that it was completely different from what preceded and what followed it. Even in a dynamic view of history, periodization may prove a very useful instrument if properly handled. The gradual changes brought about by a continuous historical development may be in large part changes in degree, but when they have progressed far enough they become for all practical purposes changes in kind. To follow a good humanist precedent and argue from the analogy of the human body, the gradual growth of man from childhood to maturity is an unbroken process, yet there is a recognizable difference between the man and the child he has been. Perhaps the analogy, as applied to the Middle Ages and the Renaissance, is unfortunate in that it suggests a value judgment that might be regarded as invidious. However that may be, it is my contention that by about the beginning of the fourteenth century in Italy and somewhat later in the North those elements in society which had set the tone of medieval culture had perceptibly lost their dominant position and thereafter gradually gave way to more recently developed forces. These, while active in the earlier period, had not been the determining factors in the creation of medieval culture but were to be the most influential in shaping the culture of the Renaissance.

That somewhat involved statement brings me to the hazardous question of what were the fundamental differences between medieval and Renaissance civilization, and to the approach to the problem which I have found most generally satisfactory. It is an approach suggested by the work of the recent economic historians who have called attention to the dynamic influence of the revival of trade, urban life, and money economy in the midst of the agrarian feudal society of the high Middle Ages. Unfortunately, economic historians have seldom spared much thought for the development of intellectual and aesthetic culture, having been content to leave that to the specialists, while, on the other hand, the historians whose special interest was religion, philosophy, literature, science, or art have all too frequently striven to explain the developments in these fields without correlating them with changes in the economic, social, and political structure of society. In the past few years, however, historians have become increasingly aware of the necessity of including all forms of human activity in any general synthesis, an awareness illustrated by Myron Gilmore's recent volume on *The World of Humanism*.[38] Further, there has been a growing tendency to find the original motive forces of historical development in basic alterations of the economic, political, and social system, which in time exert a limiting and directing influence upon intellectual interests, religious attitudes, and cultural forms. As applied to the Renaissance, this tendency has been evident in the work of several historians, notably, Edward P. Cheyney, Ferdinand Schevill, Eugenio Garin, Hans Baron, and some of the contributors to the *Propyläen Weltgeschichte*.[39]

To state my point as briefly as possible, and therefore more dogmatically than I could wish:[40] let us begin with the axiomatic premise that the two essential elements in medieval civilization were the feudal system and the universal church. The latter represented an older tradition than feudalism, but in its external structure and in many of its ideals and ways of thought it had been forced to adapt itself to the conditions of feudal society. And feudalism in turn was shaped by the necessity of adapting all forms of social and political life to the limitations of an agrarian and relatively moneyless economy. Into this agrarian feudal society the revival of commerce and industry, accompanied by the growth of towns and money economy, introduced a new and alien element. The first effect of this was to stimulate the existing medieval civilization, freeing it from the economic, social, and cultural restrictions that an almost exclusive dependence upon agriculture had imposed upon it, and making possible a rapid development in every branch of social and cultural activity. That the twelfth and thirteenth centuries were marked by the growth of a very vigorous culture no longer needs to be asserted. They witnessed the recovery of much ancient learning, the creation of scholastic philosophy, the rise of vernacular literatures and of Gothic art, perhaps on the whole a greater advance than was achieved in the two following centuries. Nevertheless, it seems to me that, despite new elements and despite rapid development, the civilization of these two centuries remained in form and spirit predominantly feudal and ecclesiastical.

But medieval civilization, founded as it was upon a basis of land tenure and agriculture, could not continue indefinitely to absorb an expanding urban society and money economy without losing its essential character, without gradually changing into something recognizably different. The changes were most obvious in the political sphere, as feudalism gave way before the rise of city states or centralized territorial states under princes who were learning to utilize the power of money. The effect upon the church was almost equally great. Its universal authority was shaken by the growing power of the national states, while its internal organization was transformed by the evolution of a monetary fiscal system which had, for a time, disastrous effects upon its moral character and prestige.[41] Meanwhile, within the cities the growth of capital was bringing significant changes in the whole character of urban economic and social organizations, of which not the least significant was the appearance of a growing class of urban laymen who had the leisure and means to secure a liberal education and to take an active part in every form of intellectual and aesthetic culture.

Taking all these factors together, the result was an essential change in the character of European civilization. The feudal and ecclesiastical elements, though still strong, no longer dominated, and they were themselves more or less transformed by the changing conditions. The culture of the period we call the Renaissance was predominantly and increasingly the product of the cities, created in major part by urban laymen whose social environment, personal habits, and professional interests were different from those of the feudal and clerical aristocracy who had largely dominated the culture of the Middle Ages. These urban laymen, and with them the churchmen who were recruited from their midst as the medieval clergy had been recruited from the landed classes, did not break suddenly or completely with their inherited traditions, but they introduced new materials and restated the old in ways that reflected a different manner of life. The Renaissance, it seems to me, was essentially an age of transition, containing much that was still medieval, much that was recognizably modern, and, also, much that, because of the mixture of medieval and modern elements, was peculiar to itself and was responsible for its contradictions and contrasts and its amazing vitality.

This interpretation of the Renaissance leaves many of the old controversial points unanswered, though a partial answer to most of them is implied in it. It may be as well not to attempt to answer all questions with a single formula. There was certainly enough variety in the changing culture of western Europe during both the Middle Ages and the Renaissance to provide historians with material to keep them happily engaged in controversy for some time to come. All that can be claimed for the approach I have suggested is that it seems to offer the broadest basis for periodization, that it points to the most fundamental differences between the civilization of the Renaissance and the Middle Ages, while recognizing the dynamic character of both. At the same time, by suggesting a broad theory of causation in the gradual transformation of the economic and social structure of western Europe, it tends to reduce the controversial questions regarding the primary influence of the classical revival, of the Italian genius, Germanic blood, medieval French culture, or Franciscan mysticism to a secondary, if not irrelevant, status. Finally, such an approach to the problem might make it possible to take what was genuinely illuminating in Burckhardt, without the exaggerations of the classical-rational-Hegelian tradition, and also without the necessity of attacking the Renaissance *per se* in attacking Burckhardtian orthodoxy.

NOTES

1. For an account of the varying interpretations of the Renaissance since the fifteenth century, see W. K. Ferguson, *The Renaissance in Historical Thought, Five Centuries of Interpretation* (Boston, 1948).

2. Petrarch, *Epistolae de rebus familiaribus*, VI, 2, ed. F. Fracassetti (Florence, 1859), I, 314.

3. F. Biondo, *Historiarum ab inclinatione Romanorum imperii decades* (Basel, 1531), p. 4.

4. See, for example, Leonardo Bruni, *Historiarum Florentini populi libri xii*, in Muratori, XIX, 3 (new ed. by E. Santini, Città di Castello, 1914).

5. Bruni, *Vite di Dante e del Petrarca*, in *Autobiografie e vite de' maggiori scrittori italiani*, ed. A. Solerti (Milan, 1903), pp. 115 ff.

6. See, for example, Erasmus, *Antibarbarorum liber* (Basel, 1520); cf. Ferguson,"Renaissance Tendencies in the Religious Thought of Erasmus," *Journal of the History of Ideas*, XV (1954), 506 ff.

7. P. Melanchthon, *De Luthero et aetatibus ecclesiae, Opera*, ed. C. G. Brettschneider (Halle, 1834-60), XI, 786.

8. J. Bale, *Illustrium maioris Britanniae scriptorum summarium* (Ipswich, 1548), f. 4^v.

9. J. Foxe, *Acts and Monuments of the Christian Martyrs* (London, 1877), III, 718 ff.; IV, 4 ff., 252 ff.

10. T. de Bèze, *Histoire ecclésiastique des Églises Réformées au royaume de France* (Paris, 1883-89), I, 5.

11. G. Vasari, *Le vite de' piu eccellenti architetti, pittori, e scultori italiani da Cimabue insino a tempi nostri* (Florence, 1550).

12. D. Hume, *History of England from the Invasion of Julius Caesar to the Revolution in 1688* (London, 1864), II, 365.

13. E. Gibbon, *The History of the Decline and Fall of the Roman Empire*, ed. J. B. Bury (New York, 1914), VII, 135 f.

14. Voltaire, *Oeuvres complètes* (Paris, 1883-85), XXIV, 548.

15. Voltaire, *Essai sur les moeurs et l'esprit des nations, Oeuvres*, XII, 123.

16. *Ibid.*, XII, 169.

17. J. Michelet, *Histoire de France*, Vol. VII: *La Renaissance* (Paris, 1855).

18. J. Burckhardt, *Die Cultur der Renaissance in Italien* (Basel, 1860).

19. P. Sabatier, *Vie de St. François d'Assise* (Paris, 1894).

20. See, for example, É. Gebhardt, *L'Italie mystique, histoire de la Renaissance religieuse au Moyen Age* (Paris, 1890); K. Burdach, *Vom Mittelalter zur Reformation* (Halle, 1893); H. O. Taylor, *Thought and Expression in the Sixteenth Century* (New York, 1920); A. von Martin, *Mittelalterliche Welt-und Lebensanschauung im Spiegel der Schriften Coluccio Salutatis*

(Munich, 1913); E. Walser, *Gesammelte Studien zur Geistesgeschichte der Renaissance* (Basel, 1932); G. Toffanin, *Storia dell'umanesimo* (Naples, 1933); and D. Bush, *The Renaissance and English Humanism* (Toronto, 1939).

21. A. Renaudet, *Préréforme et humanisme à Paris pendant les premières guerres d'Italie* (Paris, 1916).

22. P. Mestwerdt, *Die Anfänge des Erasmus: Humanismus und "Devotio Moderna"* (Leipzig, 1917); A. Hyma, *The Christian Renaissance* (New York, 1924).

23. C. Neumann, "Byzantinische Kultur und Renaissancekultur," *Historische Zeitschrift*, XCI (1903), 215-232.

24. See L. C. L. Courajod, *Leçons professées à l'École du Louvre (1887-96)*, 3 vols. (Paris, 1899-1903); H. Fierens-Gevaert, *La Renaissance septentrionale et les premiers maîtres de Flandres* (Brussels, 1905).

25. See Ferguson, *Renaissance in Historical Thought*, pp. 329 ff.

26. C. H. Haskins, *The Renaissance of the Twelfth Century* (Cambridge, 1927); F. von Bezold, *Das Fortleben der antiken Götter im mittelalterlichen Humanismus* (Bonn, 1922); see also R. R. Bolgar, *The Classical Heritage and its Beneficiaries* (Cambridge, 1954), pp. 183 ff.

27. H. O. Taylor, *The Medieval Mind* (New York, 1911).

28. H. Waddell, *The Wandering Scholars* (London, 1927).

29. É. Gilson, "Humanisme médiévale et Renaissance," in his *Les idées et les lettres* (Paris, 1932); J. Maritain, *True Humanism* (New York, 1938).

30. L. Thorndyke, *Science and Thought in the Fifteenth Century* (New York, 1929), pp. 1-10; G. Sarton, "Science in the Renaissance," in J. W. Thompson, G. Rowley, F. Schevill, and G. Sarton (eds.), *The Civilization of the Renaissance* (Chicago, 1929), p. 76.

31. J. W. Thompson, *The Literacy of the Laity in the Middle Ages* (Berkeley, 1939).

32. J. Nordström, *Moyen Age et Renaissance* (Paris, 1933).

33. See J. Huizinga, *The Waning of the Middle Ages* (London, 1924).

34. See, for example, H. Besseler, *Die Musik des Mittelalters und der Renaissance* (Potsdam, 1931-35); G. Reese, *Music in the Renaissance* (New York, 1954); A. Einstein, *The Italian Madrigal*, 3 vols. (New York, 1949); E. Lowinsky, "Music in the Culture of the Renaissance," *American Historical Review*, LIX (1953), 19 ff., and numerous other articles.

35. E. Panofsky, *Early Netherlandish Painting* (Cambridge, 1953), etc.

36. See especially E. Cassirer, *Individuum und Kosmos in der Philosophie der Renaissance* (Leipzig, 1927); P. O. Kristeller, *The Philosophy of Ficino* (New York, 1943), and numerous articles.

37. G. Mattingly, *Renaissance Diplomacy* (Boston, 1955).

38. M. Gilmore, *The World of Humanism, 1453-1517* (New York, 1952).

39. See, for example, E. P. Cheyney, *The Dawn of a New Era, 1250-1453* (New York, 1936); F. Schevill, *History of Florence from the Founding of the City through the Renaissance* (New York, 1936); E. Garin, *L'Umanesimo italiano: Filosofia e vita civele nel Rinascimento* (Bari, 1952); H. Baron, *The Crisis of the Early Italian Renaissance: Civic Humanism and Republican Liberty in an Age of Classicism and Tyranny* (Princeton, 1955); W. Goetz (ed.), *Propyläen Weltgeschichte*, Vol. IV: *Das Zeitalter der Gotik und Renaissance* (Berlin, 1932).

40. For fuller discussion, see Ferguson, "The Interpretation of the Renaissance: Suggestions for a Synthesis," *Journal of the History of Ideas*, XII (1951), 483-495.

41. For fuller discussion of this interpretation of the effect of social and economic change on state and church during the Renaissance, see Ferguson, "Toward the Modern State," in *The Renaissance, a Symposium* (New York, 1953), and "The Church in a Changing World: A Contribution to the Interpretation of the Renaissance," *American Historical Review*, LIX (1953), 1-18.

GARRETT MATTINGLY ∾ *Changing Attitudes towards the State during the Renaissance*

T HARDLY NEEDS SAYING THAT THE TITLE I CHOSE for this lecture, "Changing attitudes towards the state during the Renaissance," is both vague and presumptuous. Although a lot of people are willing to talk about the Renaissance, it is a term which has no very precise meaning. Historians and philologists, art critics and philosophers are likely to use it differently according to the special interests of their different trades, and to disagree about its scope and meaning not only as between one discipline and another, but among fellow craftsmen within each. It is even possible for some distinguished scholars to deny that there ever was such a thing as the Renaissance at all.[1]

As to attitudes toward the state—how does one define them? How certain can one ever be of what was in the minds and hearts of men now five centuries dead? And how does one decide which of these guessed-at thoughts and feelings to pick out as typical of the spirit of that bygone time and which to ignore? All these are risky matters. And they grow more risky still if one is so foolish as to pass over the formulas of professional thinkers in search of the ill-defined attitudes of the world of action. Poets, chroniclers, orators and politicians take less care of logical distinctions than the schoolmen do. The sequence of their thinking is rarely arranged in a flawless sorites and most of them are quite capable of believing at least two contradictory things at the same time. Nevertheless it is possible to argue that what goes on in the muddled minds and sentimental hearts of the general run of mankind for whom the poets and the politicians speak is often more influential on what happens, and therefore from one point of view more interesting, than what technical philosophers say on academic platforms. At any rate, with your indulgence, I shall take the risk of speaking, this evening, as if that were so. In what follows I want to examine less the explicit development of political philosophy than the shifting tides of popular judgment and sentiment by which that development was swayed.

That leaves the time of the change, the period which we had better call "the Renaissance," still to be defined. As we were saying a minute ago, the Renaissance is an elastic term. Its boundaries have often been expanded or contracted to meet the needs of a particular discipline or a particular argument, and there seems to be no good reason not to take advantage of this customary liberty. So, a narrower limit need not imply the slightest criticism of those who, with Professor Wallace Ferguson, would embrace the whole time span 1300-1600 in the Renaissance,[2] or even of those bolder spirits who, like Professor Arnold Toynbee, would thrust its boundaries back to the mid-eleventh century or forward beyond the threshold of the nineteenth.[3] (Indeed, I reserve the right to take similar liberties myself if, at some future time, it turns out to be convenient.) Now, however, I propose to limit our period to the fifteenth century plus a few decades added at either end. That period, from not long before the death of Petrarch to the sack of Rome, is what anyone who recognizes the term at all would call the Italian Renaissance. And it is just in that period, and mainly in Italy, that I think we can see a change in people's attitude towards the state, a change that was to be of the greatest significance for the future of our Western civilization.

The clearest evidence of change is that one searches in vain through the literatures of western Europe in the centuries before 1500 for any use of the word "state" in anything like its ordinary modern political meaning.[4] This is not to say that the heirs of Greece and Rome lacked organized governments or the terms in which to talk about them, or that the various forms of civil polity and their relations with one another and with the society which contained them were not matters of acute interest, eagerly discussed. But the most general term under which we subsume all the varieties of polity was lacking. In the documents of chanceries, the pamphlets of publicists, the tractates and opinions of legal luminaries, we hear of "empire," "kingdom," "lordship" and a bewildering variety of other terms for political bodies, but whenever we meet *status* or one of its cognates in the vulgar tongues it does not mean a political unit at all. "Status," "état," "stato," "estado," "state" all just meant condition, standing, dignity, one's position in society.[5] The king kept his state in his palace, but also the baron kept his state in his hall, the abbot in his monastery and the merchant in his countinghouse. In more abstract discourse, men in medieval times talked not about "states" but about "estates," the ordered ranks of society which combined, usually three or more of them together, to make up particular realms, and the totality of which composed the mystic body of Christendom.

Perhaps the men of the Middle Ages lacked our word "state" because they lacked our thing. The actual political structure they knew was a crazy quilt of overlapping jurisdictions, feudal, ecclesiastical, dynastic, corporate. A great prince like the duke of Burgundy might hold some of his dominions in fief of the king of France and the rest of his lands of the emperor, and in theory be sovereign in none of them, though in practice so powerful that emperor and king together would hesitate to cross him.[6] In a great city like Paris there might be, even under the most powerful of the Valois, more than a score of separate liberties, and legal circumscriptions, in some of which the king's decrees and the king's officers were powerless, even when the king was in his palace of the Louvre.[7] There were so many disputes about suzerainty and allegiance, so many conflicting claims to towns and provinces and whole kingdoms that though men always knew what their estate was, they could often be in grave doubt what "state" (in our modern sense of the term) they belonged to.

The ordinary way of trying to make sense of this confusion of mutually contradictory privileges and obligations, of hereditary rights and corporate liberties, or multiple and conflicting allegiances was to think of the entities involved not as a congeries of discrete, autonomous powers, but as members or aspects of one hierarchically ordered society. The order of secular rulers, the nobles, the second estate, rose from simple gentlemen through knights and barons and dukes and kings to the shadowy figure of the emperor. The order of spiritual leaders reared beside them a similar pyramid through priest and monk, bishop and abbot to the refulgent figure of the pope. Even the third estate, the broad base of the twin pyramids, was thought of as hierarchically ordered. Serfs and day-laborers worked the franklin's[8] fields, apprentices and journeymen obeyed their masters, children obeyed their parents, and wives obeyed their husbands. (I put in that last to remind you that this is a purely theoretical picture. Reality was rather different.)

From the middle of the eleventh century to beyond the middle of the fourteenth, the most difficult questions for political theory had to do with the relations between the two pyramids: between Church and State, we would say, though none of the thinkers who then grappled with the problem would have put it like that. They saw it rather as a question of the relationship between the secular and spiritual powers of one indivisible society. It was the easier for them to think of it in that way since the actual political conflict which occasioned the bulk of their writings was fought out in Italy and Germany between the popes who claimed to be, and became increasingly in fact, the spiritual rulers of Western society, and the Holy Roman Emperors who claimed to be its temporal sovereigns, and who did in fact maintain themselves, however precariously, as the feudal overlords and usually as the effective rulers of the area of conflict for almost two centuries after their power was challenged by Pope Gregory VII.[9]

Of the many contending voices in the long argument which accompanied the clash of armies in the Lombard plain and on the roads to Rome, and lasted on after the imperial power had been reduced to a wraith and the papal one was huddled in a fortress beside the strange waters of the Rhone, we remember today chiefly two. One is Dante's impassioned plea for the supremacy of the Emperor, because to achieve its highest goals civilization needs one thing above all, universal peace, and peace can only be maintained by one single, universally recognized authority, ready to judge and to enforce judgment with the sword.[10] The other voice, earlier in time than Dante's, softer, more moderate but not less unshakeable in its certainty, is that of St. Thomas, insisting that man's highest goal is not health or wealth, knowledge or even virtue but the grace of God, so that in a Christian society kings and even the Emperor must be subject to the Vicar of that Grace.[11]

There were many other voices. Early in their struggle with the emperors, the popes had encouraged the kings of Europe to reject any claim of imperial suzerainty and to consider themselves, in effect, emperors in their own domains.[12] Later on, in at least three of these kingdoms, England, France, and Castile, some of the wearers of these crowns and their servants began to take their claims to *imperium* pretty seriously, and to grow restive at what they considered papal interference with their affairs. They were more successful in asserting their independence than the emperors had been, and, in the course of their quarrels with the papacy, they found spokesmen who made claims for their authority within the narrow limits of their hereditary provinces just as uncompromising as the old universal claims of pope and emperor had been.[13]

From one point of view these literary gladiators for the late medieval kings may be seen as the first chauvinists, or, if you

prefer, as the first exponents of national sovereignty. Their assertions of the freedom of the kings they served from any exterior
controls really did foreshadow the coming disintegration of medieval society. But of this none of them, as far as one can tell, had
any idea. All of them, apparently, assumed the unity of Latin
Christendom as confidently and incuriously as had St. Thomas or
Dante. The myth or fiction of the *Respublica Christiana*, of the
unitary, hierarchically ordered society in which every individual,
every corporation, every people had its appointed place, and
which everyone from emperor and pope to villein and serf was
meant to guard and serve, continued to be basic to their political
thinking, even while they prized away at its foundations.[14] And
all of them, with perhaps no more than a single exception, seem
to have evaluated the parts of that society, as St. Thomas and
Dante did, teleologically. They judged the behavior of persons
and the functioning of institutions in terms of the purpose they
were meant to serve, and they criticized these several purposes in
terms of the all-embracing purpose, the final end of the great
society itself.

A fifteenth century archbishop of Toulouse, one Bernard du
Rosier, offers us a good example. In his later years Bishop Bernard
was one of the servants of Charles the Well-Served, and among
his surviving but unpublished works there is a discourse on the
antiquity, dignity, and general pre-eminence of the French monarchy which makes up in enthusiasm for whatever it may lack in
historical accuracy or literary polish. The good bishop is of interest here because, besides his special pleading for the French monarchy and the Gallican church, he also wrote a little book, a
Brevilogus[15] about ambassadors, and ambassadors make especially
good test cases for attitudes toward the state. That is because
ambassadors often find themselves in situations which clearly ex-
pose any conflict between their duty to their government and the
prevailing moral code. Bishop Bernard had been an ambassador
himself, and he was quite aware of the moral dilemmas which
might confront a diplomat on mission. But because of his basic

assumptions, the difficulties do not seem so acute as they were to become, and he does not hesitate in his solution. His first premise is that every ambassador is a public official. This seems so obvious that at first the modern reader fails to see that what the bishop is saying is not what we think at all, but something strange and rather shocking. He does not mean that an ambassador is a public servant because he has received credentials and expects to draw pay from a particular prince or republic. On the contrary, no matter whose subject he may be, or who may have given him his credentials, the ambassador, in virtue of his office, is the servant of a much larger public, in fact, of the whole of human society or, at the very least, of the common corps of Christendom, of the *Respublica Christiana*, in which all the nations and governments of the Latin west are mystically united.

So, the standard by which an ambassador must determine his conduct on every occasion is quite clear. He is an officer of the great society. The chief worldly good of that society is peace. It is exactly to serve that end that the ambassador's office exists. So, the business of any ambassador is peace. He must do everything to advance that end, nothing to endanger it. Presumably, the prince whose credentials he bears also wants peace, or he would not have employed an ambassador. At any rate the ambassador must assume so. For if he acts in any other way, plotting treason or rebellion or stirring up war, he must not expect to escape the punishment he so richly deserves.

Now all this, mind you, is not the dreamy idealism of some isolated utopian philosopher. It is an emphatic piece of advice taken from a practical handbook for diplomats written by a man who was himself a practical diplomat, administrator, and politician. It only says in simpler language what all the jurists of the period were saying about the rights and duties of ambassadors. And the maxims of the jurists, no matter how unrealistic their assumptions may sound to us, really did represent the accepted legal rules and ordinary norms of conduct of the period we have been talking about.[16] Actual forms of political organization were changing, and changing conditions brought changing modes of behavior. But people's minds change more slowly than their environment. So, throughout most of Europe, right up to the year 1500 and beyond, most people went on thinking in terms of the hierarchically ordered great society and passing judgments on its parts in terms of how proper they were for that society's overriding final ends. As long as they did so their attitude towards the state was bound to be so different from that of modern times that they can hardly be said to have possessed the concept of the state at all.

There were, of course, exceptions, getting more numerous as our period drew towards its close. But in all the fourteenth century I know of only one, though an outstanding one surely, Marsiglio of Padua. He wrote a book called *Defensor Pacis*, "The Defender of the Peace," a part of the interminable battle of words between pope and emperor, a book finished about 1324, perhaps no more than a decade or so after Dante's contribution, and within three years after Dante's death. Superficially the two books, Marsiglio's and Dante's, are much alike. Both are antipapal and proimperial. Both base themselves on Aristotle. Both make a main point of the maintenance of peace by the civil authority. And both (this is not negligible) are by Italians. On analysis, it would be hard to find two books on the same side of the same question more different. Dante's *De Monarchia* looks back nostalgically to an irrevocable past, a past already beyond the realm of the possible before Dante was born. Marsiglio's *Defensor Pacis* looks forward, or seems to look forward to the modern, omnicompetent, sovereign state. No matter how much of argument and actual language Marsiglio may have borrowed from his predecessors (and he seems to have borrowed a good deal)[17] his mood, his attitude, the emphasis of his arguments are likely to remind the ordinary reader far more of Machiavelli or even of Hobbes than of Gregory of Catino or Pierre Dubois. The monarchy Dante is talking of is universal. This is its whole point. The peace it is meant to insure is peace among princes and peoples, the peace of the world. Marsiglio knew very well that the emperor was not a universal monarch and that there was no universal monarchy. The state he was talking about, *civitas* he calls it, or sometimes *civitas sive regnum*, could be any existing kingdom or city state at all, Hungary, Naples, Bohemia, Venice, Milan, or his own Padua.[18] The peace Marsiglio aims at is internal, domestic peace, for he sees the city or kingdom not as an ideal moral and intellectual community, a perfect society, self-sufficing and indestructible, but as a government imposed by men upon men and hovering precariously on the brink of destruction. Therefore Marsiglio is not concerned with ends but with means. His preoccupation, like Machiavelli's, is not with moral or religious ideals, but with how to preserve and strengthen an existing state.[19]

For once Padua proved a better teacher of politics than Florence. When Marsiglio was growing up there, the town was a vigorous city republic with wide participation by its more substantial citizens in the affairs of government, a republic periodically convulsed like most of its neighbors by class and factional strife, but bustling with life and proud of its free institutions. In those days the Paduan republicans would yield no jot of their independence, not even to pope or emperor, and were reaching out, like the greedy rivals all round them, for whatever weaker towns might be swept within their grasp. Before Marsiglio sought the court of the Emperor Lewis the Bavarian, where he wrote his famous book, Padua under the strain of foreign war and domestic unrest had already given itself into the hands of a dictator, Jacopo da Carrara, the founder of a dynasty which lasted there almost a century. It was probably from watching the political drama of Padua and its neighbors in the troubled Lombard plain that Marsiglio began to discern the shape of a new kind of state.

Indeed, the city states of northern and central Italy, whether republics or despotisms, were a new political phenomenon in Christendom. In the hierarchically ordered structure of the Latin west, they were an anomaly without real parallel. Superficially, they were more like the city-states of the antique Mediterranean

world than anything else, and this surface resemblance had a
good deal to do with the enthusiasm of their inhabitants for the
art and literature of Greece and Rome. But fundamentally they
were a different type of organism, one never seen in the world
before. They were unique because they were the product of a
unique revolution, the revolution of the religious radicals among
the clergy of the West led by the popes against the Holy Roman
Emperors and the social order they represented. The object of
that revolution was to break the ties which held the Church in
bondage to the feudal system. The militia of the revolution, its
chief fighting strength in Italy, was the citizenry of the Italian
communes, roused by popular evangelists or by the reformers
among their parish priests. Because the emperor's barons in their
castles lorded it over the countryside, and the emperor's bishops
ruled the cities in his name, the militia of the revolution had to
begin by smashing their way out of subjection to both the feudal
and the ecclesiastical hierarchies. The barons' castles were pulled
down and the nobles were made to live in the city and be subject
to its laws. The bishops were stripped of their secular powers and
only allowed to enter their own cathedrals if they would submit
to municipal controls. By the time the popes noticed what was
happening, it was too late to reverse the trend, and anyway, right
up to the death of the Emperor Frederick II in 1250, the papacy
needed the support of the towns in its death struggle with the
empire.

So, by a paradox, a clerical revolution produced in Italy the
first, and for a long time the only, purely secular states in Europe.[20]
Everywhere else, temporal powers were masked and sanctified by
religious forms and immemorial customs. Elsewhere, kings,
anointed with holy oils and crowned by high priests with special,
sacred ceremonies, ruled in accordance with laws considered to
be eternal over intricately interconnected segments of the great
society. But in Italy, the city republics were temporal powers in
the purest sense of the word. The kind of freedom they had won
left them without even the most tenuous connection with eter-

nity. Like the beasts that perish, their welfare and their survival depended on their cunning and their strength.

Just as political life in the Italian cities was precarious to a degree unknown in the legitimate monarchies and chartered communes beyond the Alps, so it was proportionally more self-conscious. In each city the party, the social class, the tyrant temporarily in power had climbed there by force or craft and had to stay there by the same means. Always, whether the city was Guelph or Ghibelline, democracy, oligarchy, or tyranny, there were enemies hovering not far without the gates. Internecine fears and hatreds within the walls made exiles, at any given moment, of a substantial number of the prominent citizens of every Italian city, and since the nearest independent city was almost certain to be hostile, and likely, out of rivalry, to wear a different party color, exiles usually found a convenient refuge nearby from which to plot their return, just as they usually found accomplices in conspiracy among their fellow citizens still at home. Even when one dominant family had crushed all opposition within a city, the poison of illegitimate power turned son against father and brother against brother with horrifying frequency.

Under such circumstances, just to *mantenere lo stato*—to keep a grip on the government, that is—to uphold the status of the people currently in power, was a painful, continuous problem. Balanced precariously over destruction and jabbed at by enemies from all directions, the men in power had little leisure to reflect on ideal ends. They had to think about immediate means. From the angle of their preoccupations Marsiglio of Padua first approached the main questions of politics, thus breaking with the traditions of the schoolmen. And it was in the same context and with preference to the same critical point: "How to keep the government running and how to keep running the government" (*Come mantenere lo stato?*) that the word from which our modern term "state" was soon to be developed first enters discussions of political theory.

Throughout the fourteenth century, educated Italians were a little uneasy in the presence of these new, unsanctified temporal states. The lawyers did their not very effective best to provide some sort of rationalization which would assimilate the revolutionary communes to the established and acknowledged order of Christendom,[21] just as their rulers, tyrants or oligarchs, tended to buy titles or charters from popes and emperors as patents of respectability. Meanwhile the earliest humanists, Petrarch and his friends and disciples, were troubled and ambivalent.[22] They were stirred by the civic patriotism of their Latin forefathers. They were entangled, often, in the thicket of fierce loves and passionate hatreds which was the politics of their own time. They responded with full sympathy to the vaulting amb⟨ition⟩ and implacable resentments of their contemporaries. B⟨ut⟩ ⟨li⟩ke the Petrarch of the letter to Cicero, they were inclined to feel that a man careful of his soul should not bow down to secular idols or let the service of worldly ends, however unselfish, draw his thoughts too far from God. Besides, over all their political thinking lay the shadow of the power exalted by Dante, the power that Paul had appealed to and Christ Himself had acknowledged, the chilling shadow of Caesar.

Then, as a brilliant book[23] has recently shown, just at the turn of the century a new spirit quickened in Florence. The occasion was the successful resistance of the Florentine republic against the efforts of the tyrant Duke of Milan, Giangaleazzo Visconti, to make himself lord of Italy. One by one the allies of Florence deserted her. One by one the last city republics of Italy surrendered their liberties to the great Duke, until Florence stood alone, surrounded and at bay. Giangaleazzo ordered his crown and began to arrange the ceremonies of his coronation as King of Italy. To the desperate Florentines, the great comet which flamed across the heavens in the spring of 1402 must have seemed to portend the death of Italian freedom. Instead it announced the death of the great Duke.[24] Florence was saved, and her people felt a swift surge of pride. When all their neighbors had chosen

peace and safety at the price of submission, they had chosen freedom, in spite of terrible dangers, and God had averted the dangers
and preserved their freedom. Their faith in the republic was
confirmed.

The death of Giangaleazzo marked a decisive turn in the political development of Italy. After his failure, no one was to come
so near again to unifying the wealthy and civilized regions of the
peninsula. For the next century Italy would be divided among a
number of city states, each ruling its surrounding territory, and
some of them, at least, precociously like the territorial states of
Europe at a much later period.[25] And from the moment of the
triumph which had determined this result, the humanists of
Florence, the intellectual leaders of Italy, took a new attitude
towards the state.[26] They began to reassert without reservation
the importance of civic virtue and the duty of public service as
once asserted by Cicero and Livy and the other encomiasts of the
Roman republic. Love of the little fatherland, a special piety and
pride towards one's own city, was already strong in Italy. Was
it ever absent in any Mediterranean civilization? One thinks of
the eleventh century Pisan poet celebrating his city's triumph
over the Saracens,[27] and of the proud verses on the great stairway
of the town hall at Toledo.[28] Now to this primitive patriotism
there was added a self-conscious acknowledgment of the supreme
claim of one's city to loyalty and devotion deliberately modelled
on the classical worship of *Roma Dea*. The result was a set of
values and a code of conduct as potent in inspiring disinterested
service to the state as the code of chivalry had ever been in insur-
ing fealty to a feudal overlord.

In fact, the conscious imitation of Greece and Rome in political
feeling meant a long step in the direction of substituting the religion of patriotism for the religion of Christ. But at first that
was by no means obvious. In Florence, and later in Venice, it
was the republican and antimonarchical component of the classicizing attitude which attracted immediate attention. Except in
Rome, where the republican sentiments of the humanists flavored

the conspiracy of Stefano Porcaro against Pope Nicholas V,[29] and the later vaporings of the Academy,[30] there was nothing in this classicizing patriotism which was necessarily anti-Christian or even anticlerical. When, for instance, Filippo Maria Visconti replied to the papal thunders of Eugenius IV that he valued his soul more than his body but his state more than either, men could take the declaration either as a blasphemous joke or a jocular blasphemy. Either way, nothing was implied about any general attitude; nothing was revealed but Filippo Maria's own enormous egotism. His "state" was that of tyrant of Milan. If he had used the word in that sense, he could have said with far more justice than Louis XIV, "I am the state." Nevertheless the Visconti tyrant's defiant proclamation of his preference of his political aims above his soul's salvation did come at a moment in the renewed power struggle when other men besides princes were being forced to a similar choice. For the more savagely the Italian states struggled against each other for power, the clearer it became that a man's duty to his country or his prince might run counter to what had always been counted the primary duties of a Christian and a gentleman.

The possible contradiction was clearest in diplomacy. An ambassador had two main duties: to represent the views and advance the interests of the prince or republic he served, and to care for the larger interests of that Christian commonwealth whose officer he was. Even before the power struggle had become as continuous and intensive as it was in fifteenth century Italy, even before diplomacy had become mainly a bridge between one war and the next, men had seen that these two duties might not always pull the same way. In practice, diplomats had solved the dilemma sometimes one way, sometimes another, but in precept and theory there was only one accepted solution, that set forth by Bernard du Rosier. An ambassador is an officer of the Republic of Christendom. Therefore the business of an ambassador is peace. All his advice to his own government and his negotiations with that to which he is sent should be to that end. Since the greater interest includes the less, he must not act contrary to that greater interest, even at the express order of his prince.

Then, towards the end of the fifteenth century, a Venetian diplomat and humanist, Ermolao Barbaro wrote the first treatise on diplomacy to ignore all these medieval precepts and to proceed on quite contrary assumptions. Ermolao did not say, "The ambassador is the servant of all"; or "The ambassador works for the common good"; but "The business of the ambassador, like that of any other civil servant, is to do, say, advise and think only whatever may best serve the preservation and aggrandizement of his own state."[31] No other consideration, no private scruple of mind or heart may obstruct the performance of this duty. Until public policy has been decided on, the ambassador is free, and indeed has a duty, to urge the course of action which he thinks most advantageous for the state. But once a line of policy has been fixed, the ambassador must do everything in his power to help carry it out, no matter how distasteful it may be to his convictions or his sentiments. In diplomacy, Ermolao makes it clear, private morality must give place to public advantage, and, for Venetians, the interests of the republic of Venice come ahead of the interests of the Republic of Christendom.

Since his little book had to wait more than four hundred years for publication, Ermolao failed to achieve the place he deserves among the first prophets of the religion of patriotism. He would have been overshadowed anyhow by another Italian diplomat, a younger contemporary of his, Niccolò Machiavelli, a Florentine. It is popular, these days, to explain that the chief distinction of Machiavelli is his complete amorality. He is represented as having thrust all considerations of morality or religion, all sentiment and all emotion out of his studies so that he might look at politics with the coolness and indifference of a scientist in a laboratory.[32] I know I am in a minority about this, and I may be wrong, but I think this modern view does the Florentine less than justice. Machiavelli—I mean the Machiavelli of the serious, major books, the *History of Florence*, the *Art of War*, and, above all, the *Dis-*

courses on the First Ten Books of Livy—that Machiavelli knew as well as Aristotle or St. Thomas or Francisco de Vitoria that politics cannot be divorced from ethics. But under the shock of a terrible experience, the collapse of the Florentine republic, to which he had given such long and faithful service and from which he had hoped so much, for Machiavelli the norm of ethical judgment had shifted. For Aristotle it was the good life, for St. Thomas the Christian life, for which the state existed. They judged the different forms of political organization by how well they served the individual's highest good, just as Vitoria judged the conduct of states toward one another by the same touchstone. Machiavelli, on the other hand, was prepared to judge men, was, in fact, always judging men, by how well they served the safety and aggrandizement of the state.

Machiavelli was a man mad about the state. He could, so he once confessed to a friend, talk about nothing else.[33] He is even credited, sometimes, with being the first writer to popularize the word—*lo stato*—in something like our modern meaning. This is, of course, in part an illusion. Our meaning carries connotations of Cromwell and Louis XIV and Frederick of Prussia, of Rousseau and the French Revolution and the philosophy of Hegel, of which, perforce, Machiavelli was innocent. In compensation, he knew one thing now almost forgotten. He knew that the state, that reified abstraction, never really does anything. It is people who do things, using the machinery of the state. That, indeed, is essentially what *lo stato* seems to have meant to Machiavelli: the levers of power, the machinery of government. Yet it is not without significance that Machiavelli's prose has given trained scholars the illusion that they found in it the word "state" used as they used it themselves.[34] The bond of sympathy sprang from the fact that Machiavelli shared many of our typical modern attitudes towards the state. Of these, one in particular is basic. Today almost everyone takes it for granted, but in the sixteenth century Machiavelli alone clearly expressed it. He looked to the state for salvation.

Machiavelli despaired of men left to their own resources with a more than Augustinian despair. It was not just that men were all naturally sinners. One of the things that made him impatient with them was that they were not even very good at sinning.[35] It was not so much that men were naturally evil as that he found them naturally selfish, cowardly, fickle, base, and generally worthless. And yet in the pages of the Livy he had dreamed over as a child,[36] and in the other histories of antiquity he had leisure to study in his enforced retirement there were instances of human behavior at the highest level, of courage and self-sacrifice, of justice and generosity, of wisdom and moderation, even of that rarest of human virtues, gratitude. Nor was such behavior confined to exceptional heroes and wellborn and specially trained aristocrats. Often, among the Romans, quite common people displayed these qualities, and sometimes the people as a whole.[37] The more he thought of it, the more he felt sure that what made the difference was the nature of the state. Only a strong, healthy state could make good laws and steadily enforce them. And only good laws, so long and steadily enforced that obedience to them became a habit, could ever make men good.[38]

From the corruption and depravity of his own time, Machiavelli turned wistfully to the virtues of Lycurgan Sparta and the Rome of the early republic. He knew that the Italy of his own time must be corrupt because everywhere freedom had succumbed to tyranny, because the native militia of the free Florentine republic had run like rabbits from a handful of Spanish mercenaries, because the chief executive of the republic had abdicated his powers at the first smell of danger and scuttled off to safety.[39] What Machiavelli did not know was that the writers he relied on knew almost as little of the antique republics they idealized as he did himself. But if his logic was faulty and his history mostly myth, his instinct for the trend of politics and his powers of contemporary observation were sound. Lack of political stability and military strength was reducing the brilliant civilization of Italy to misery. The future belonged to the strong states, and such states would increasingly demand the same self-sacrificing and uncritical devotion which Livy said his remote ancestors had once paid to Rome.

Machiavelli ran before the demand. He valued religions chiefly as they were useful to the state,[40] and if he could have established the antique pagan worship of the state in Florence he would have done so gladly. In the service of that idol he was prepared to condone, even to recommend, acts of cruelty and treachery such as he would have shrunk from in loathing had they been committed for private ends. He took the safety of the people for the supreme law, and the good of the state for an infallible moral guide. It is hard to make out now whether he did so because he thought that in the service of the state man found his highest good or because he thought that only powerful states could have those good laws without which men could never become good. Probably he never disentangled the two ideas, just as he certainly never asked himself how much of his acceptance of his basic assumptions was due to those operations of reason and experience that he was always praising and how much to sheer unanalyzed emotion. However that may have been, in every phase of his political writings, in his impassioned advocacy of a national militia, in his selective narrative of his country's past, in his paean to the republican virtues of ancient Rome, as in his earlier state papers, he was always preaching, now by ironic innuendo, now with angry eloquence, the new morality, the worship and service of power. He had to wait to be recognized until the nineteenth century, but by now his role is clear. He was the first great prophet of the religion of the state.

To the story of the shift of political attitudes in Renaissance Italy and the beginnings of the modern tendency to make the good of the state an independent moral absolute, there is a curious transalpine pendant. It seems absurd, at first, to suggest that Martin Luther complemented and completed Niccolò Machiavelli. It is true that both of them despaired of mankind left to its own resources, and both of them saw in the great ones of the world, spiritual and temporal, no exemption from the common proneness to evil. If some of Machiavelli's comments on the papacy and the hierarchy were translated into German and slipped into Luther's *Table Talk* they would seem quite at home there, while Brother Martin once wrote that the princes of this earth were generally its biggest fools or its wickedest knaves,[41] a judgment in which, one gathers, Machiavelli would have concurred. But beyond this the two diverged absolutely. Machiavelli could talk of nothing but politics; Luther never talked politics if he could help it. Luther expected nothing in the way of salvation from any of man's works, least of all from Machiavelli's idol, the state. In this world given over to evil the governors were not likely to be less evil than others. Usually they were, Luther would have agreed with St. Augustine, no better than great bands of robbers. At best they were God's jailers and hangmen. Governments existed because people were wicked, and most rulers seemed to have been sent by God as a special extra punishment for their subjects' sins.[42]

And yet, because good works were vain, because this world was a dark place of sin and suffering in which no real improvement was to be expected, Martin Luther exalted the state even higher than did Machiavelli.[43] Having destroyed the ecclesiastical hierarchy, he set the princes in the places of the bishops, and made the Church subordinate to the State, so that from state churches grew state-worship. He gave the prosecution of heresy into the hands of the prince and his servants, so that the state could be the jailer of men's minds as well as of their bodies. And he interpreted with complete literalness the first verses of the thirteenth chapter of Romans. "There is no power but of God: the powers that be are ordained of God. Whosoever therefore resisteth the power, resisteth the ordinance of God: and they that resist shall receive to themselves damnation." So all power partook of the divine, the Sultan's no less than the Emperor's, the wickedest tyrant's just the same as that of the most just and pious legitimate prince. Power was sanctified not by the manner of its exercise but by the mere fact that it was power, and Luther was able to counsel submission to even the worst of rulers.[44] Machiavelli would have been as shocked by that as pious Lutherans were to be shocked over the next three hundred years by the cynical advice of Machiavelli.

Between them the Florentine diplomat and the German monk illustrated and foreshadowed the change in political attitudes which marked the transition from medieval to modern times. Between them they may be said to have laid the psychological foundations of the modern state, and so of the kind of international society in which we live today. It is comforting to remember that they did so from the very highest motives.

NOTES

1. For the fullest and best discussion of this point, see W. K. Ferguson, *The Renaissance in Historical Thought* (Boston, 1948).

2. Ferguson, "The Church in a Changing World," *The American Historical Review*, LIX (1953), 1-2.

3. A. J. Toynbee, *A Study of History*, IX (London, 1954), 6 and 645-648.

4. "Stato: Storia del nome," by Felice Battaglia in *Enciclopedia Italiana* (Rome, 1936), XXXII, 613 ff.

5. Cf. Ducange; Littré; Tommaseo; *New English Dictionary;* etc. The N.E.D. finds the first use of "state" to mean a body politic in Thomas Starkey, cir. 1538 (?).

6. H. Pirenne, *Histoire de Belgique* (1922), II, *passim;* cf. P. de Commines, *Mémoires*, IV, ii and iii.

7. R. Doucet, *Les institutions de la France au XVI* e *siècle* (Paris, 1948), I, 360-395 and references there cited; F. Funck-Bretano, *Ce qu'était un roi de France* (Paris, 1950), pp. 183-184.

8. In generalizing about the Middle Ages in any language one always needs to be aware that one's choice of terms limits the scope of one's generalization. The term "franklin" in the sense used here is only appropriate to fourteenth and fifteenth century England. But other regions of Europe knew nonnoble freemen who held enough land to hire labor or command customary services.

9. For the political theorists of this struggle, see R. W. and A. J. Carlyle, *A History of Medieval Political Theory in the West*, Vols. IV and V (London, 1927).

10. Dante's *De Monarchia* (many eds.), especially Bk. I, Chs. IV and V.

11. Divi Thomae Aquinatis, *De Regimine Principum* (Turin, 1924); also in *Opera Omnia* (many eds.), especially Ch. XIV.

12. R. W. and A. J. Carlyle, V, 143; G. De Lagarde, *Recherches sur l'esprit politique de la Réforme* (Douai, 1926), pp. 63 ff.

13. R. W. and A. J. Carlyle, I, 75.

14. *Ibid.*, VI (London, 1936), 111-171, *et passim;* P. Mesnard, *L'essor de la philosophie politique au XVI* e *siècle* (Paris, 1952), pp. 91-92, 195-197; F. L. Baumer, "The Conception of Christendom in Renaissance England," *Journal of the History of Ideas*, VI (1945), 131-156.

15. Printed in V. E. Hrabar, *De Legatis et Legationibus, Tractatiis Varii* (Dorpat, 1906),

16. G. Mattingly, *Renaissance Diplomacy* (Boston, 1955), Chs. III and IV and references there cited.

17. A. Gewirth, *Marsilius of Padua and Medieval Political Philosophy* (New York, 1951), pp. 3-20, 32-44.

18. *Defensor Pacis*, I, xvii; cf. Gewirth, pp. 115-131.

19. Gewirth, pp. 85 ff.

20. Cf. E. Rosenstock-Huessy, *Out of Revolution* (New York, 1938), pp. 516-593.

21. F. Ercole, *Da Bartolo all'Althusio* (Florence, 1938), pp. 49-118.

22. H. Baron, "Cicero and the Roman Civic Spirit," *Bulletin of the John Rylands Library*, Manchester, XXII (1938), 72-97.

23. *Ibid.*, *The Crisis of the Early Italian Renaissance*, 2 vols. (Princeton, 1955).

24. N. Valeri, *L'Italia nell' eta dei principati* (Verona, 1949), pp. 291-293.

25. Baron, "Towards a More Positive Evaluation of the Fifteenth-Century Renaissance," *Journal of the History of Ideas*, IV (1943), 21 ff.

26. *Ibid.*, "The Historical Background of the Florentine Renaissance," *History*, N. S. XXII (1938), 315-327, and numerous other studies, culminating in his *The Crisis ...* (see note 23 above) and *Humanistic and Political Literature in Florence and Venice at the Beginning of the Quattrocento* (Cambridge, Mass., 1955), a complementary volume to *The Crisis*.

27. "Inclytorum Pisanorum scripturus historiam,
Antiquorum Romanorum renovo memoriam,
Nam ostendit modo Pisa laudem admirabilem,
Quam olim recepit Roma vincendo Carthaginem." Quoted by H. O. Taylor, *The Medieval Mind* (London, 1927), I, 253.

28. "Nobles discretos varones
Que gobernáis á Toledo,
En aquestos escalones
Desechad las aficiones,
Codicias, amor y miedo.
Por los comunes provechos
Dejad los particulares;
Pues os fizo Dios pilares
De tan riquisímos techos,
Estad firmes y derechos." Quoted by R. B. Merriman, *Rise of the Spanish Empire* (New York, 1918), I, 190-191.

29. L. von Pastor, *History of the Popes* (St. Louis, 1898), II, 215 ff.

30. *Ibid.*, IV, 36 ff.

31. E. Barbaro, *De officio legati*, in Hrabar, p. 66; see Mattingly, Ch. XI and references there cited.

32. The phrase is Ernst Cassirer's in *The Myth of the State* (Garden City, N.Y., 1955), pp. 192-193, but the judgment is one towards which the consensus of the twentieth century has been tending. Cf. F. Pollock, *History of the Science of Politics* (London, 1911), p. 43; Mesnard (see note 14 above), pp. 77-83.

33. Letter to Francesco Vettori, 9 April, 1513.

34. G. Condorelli in *Archivio Giuridico*, LXXXIX (1923), 223-235; F. Ercole, *La politica di Machiavelli* (Rome, 1926); etc. Since this lecture was delivered, Prof. J. H. Hexter has published in *Studies in the Renaissance*, IV (1957), a brilliant and persuasive article, pp. 113-138, dedicated to proving that, in the *Prince* anyway, Machiavelli did not mean by "stato" anything like "a political body," and that, consequently, most of his modern Italian explicators have been quite wrong.

35. *Discorsi sopra la Prima Deca di Tito Livio*, I, xxvii.

36. R. Ridolfi, *Vita di Niccolò Machiavelli* (Rome, 1954), p. 8.

37. *Discorsi*, I, lviii, xxix.

38. *Il Principe*, xii; *Discorsi*, I, l.

39. P. Villari, *The Life and Times of Niccolò Machiavelli*, trans. Linda Villari (London, 1892), II, 14-19; Ridolfi, pp. 197-198; Machiavelli, *Epigrammi*, "La notte che mori Pier Soderini."

40. *Discorsi*, I, xi-xiv.

41. "Gemeinlich die grosten narren odder die ergisten buben auf orden," *Von Weltlicher Oberkeit* (1523), in Weimar ed. XI, 267-268. In slightly varying language Luther repeated this judgment a number of times.

42. *Von Weltlicher Oberkeit*, W. XI, 272; cf. *Eine treue Vermahnung*, W. VII, 674, and *Ein Sermon von dem Bann*, W. VI, 73.

43. J. N. Figgis, *From Gerson to Grotius* (Cambridge, 1923), pp. 55-72; G. H. Sabine, *A History of Political Theory* (New York, 1937), pp. 358-362; Mesnard (see note 14 above), pp. 201 ff. For a contrary opinion (always possible about Luther) see J. W. Allen, *A History of Political Thought in the Sixteenth Century* (New York, 1928), pp. 26-30.

44. From his *Commentary on the Epistle to the Romans*, on which he was working in 1515-1516, to his death, Luther does not appear to have budged on this central point. Submission did not mean, of course, obedience in commands contrary to the word of God. The true Christian would choose martyrdom, but would not resist.

E. HARRIS HARBISON ~ *Machiavelli's* Prince *and More's* Utopia

NOTE: The lectures which Mr. Harbison offered in the Arensberg series were published in the fall of 1956 as part of his book *The Christian Scholar in the Age of the Reformation* (Scribner). The essay that follows is based on two lectures prepared for delivery on the M. D. Anderson foundation at The Rice Institute in April 1957 and published in *The Rice Institute Pamphlet*, XLIV, No. 3 (October 1957).

HE TWO WORKS OF THE RENAISSANCE MOST WIDE-ly read today are probably Niccolò Machiavelli's *Prince* and Thomas More's *Utopia*. There is good reason for this continuing popularity, even apart from the high literary qualities of both books. Machiavelli and More have come to personify the beginnings of modern political thinking. After a long period in which the leaders of thought in Europe had assumed that social institutions in general were patterned by God and so could not be made better or worse by man, Machiavelli and More appeared as the most articulate spokesmen, each in his own way, of the idea that society and the institutions composing it—not merely individuals—can be changed for the better. In different ways each stumbled upon what later became crucial problems of Western society. And so each gained the reputation of being a "prophet," a "modern," "born before his time." It is true that neither had very much influence on the technical political

theory of his own day. But their books and ideas are alive today in a way shared by very few, if any, of the other books and ideas of the period.

Between them they gave us two words which have absorbed a heavy freight of meaning in the intervening centuries: "Machiavellian" and "Utopian." And this is a measure of their stature and importance—even if Machiavelli was no "Machiavellian" and More no "Utopian"—as indeed they were not. Together they represent the first tough-minded but imaginative thinking about modern political, social, and economic problems. And together they symbolize the perennial tension between the two polar attitudes on these problems: that of the "realist" and that of the "moralist." Sometimes it is well in historical study to reflect on the familiar and well known to make sure that we understand it before we push our knowledge out further into the unknown. At any rate this essay will concern itself with these two very familiar figures and their best-known books, with a view to inquiring how "realists" and "moralists" are made, what the issue between them was in the early sixteenth century (the words of course were not used then as we use them now), and what there is of enduring significance for us in the twentieth century in this phase of Renaissance political speculation.

We may begin by recalling some of the chief contrasts and coincidences between the two men. Machiavelli was born in Florence in 1469, Thomas More in London nine years later. They never met nor (so far as we know) ever read each other's works. Machiavelli spent his earlier years in active civil service, his later years in bitter enforced retirement. More spent his early years in private life and long resisted the call to service of his king, which he entered in his later years. Machiavelli was driven to write by being dismissed from office, More (in part) by being invited to assume office. Machiavelli wrote his major works in Italian for the perusal of a few and never published them during his lifetime; More wrote his most famous book in Latin and published it immediately, to the delight of the learned all over Europe. The two wrote almost simultaneously. Machiavelli composed *The Prince* in 1513 and dedicated his final version of it to Lorenzo de' Medici in 1516, the same year More's *Utopia* came off the presses at Louvain. Machiavelli was a thorough pagan who nevertheless remained a formal Christian, saw his son enter the priesthood, and died with a priest at his bedside. More was one of the great Christians of history, who nevertheless remained a layman all his life and is remembered today as much for his more worldly qualities as for his sainthood—his humor, his family life, his zest for classical learning, and his shrewd grasp of social problems. Machiavelli died a disappointed man in 1527, before word could reach him that another man had been given the public office he had long coveted. More died triumphantly on the scaffold in 1535, "the King's good servant," as he put it, "but God's first."

Apparently then they were polar opposites. But it is important not to forget what they had in common. Each of them represented a combination, not too common even in the Renaissance, of scholarly tastes and practical experience, of humanistic accomplishment and civil service. Each was a Humanist in the contemporary sense of the word, that is, one who was convinced of the importance and relevance of classical study and who devoted much of his time to it. At the same time, each was saved from the dilettantism of many contemporary Humanists by his strong practical interests. Both believed in the efficacy of appealing to men's intelligence, but neither believed that an intellectual could change the world merely by writing books. Both wrote with exceptional simplicity, and yet both managed to set their readers to arguing violently about what they really meant to say. The major conclusion of these arguments, which are now over four centuries old, seems to be this: that Machiavelli was a "realist" with a strong streak of idealism in him, and that More was an "idealist" with a strong dash of realism. In other words, they were polar opposites, but with much in common.

The social conditions which set each of them to thinking about political problems were quite different, yet here too there was a good deal in common. Machiavelli's Italy was a far cry from More's England, but the social circumstances which underlay the birth of modern political thinking were much the same all over Europe. It is hard to describe these circumstances without grossly distorting the picture by oversimplification. The most direct way perhaps is to say that the political thought of the brilliant generation that included Machiavelli and More was the result of two things: the social tensions accompanying the dissolution of medieval institutions, and the simultaneous impact of the classical revival.

At the close of the fifteenth century the medieval *respublica christiana* was disintegrating rapidly. The pattern was still there in men's minds, the pattern of a hierarchical society headed in its temporal aspects by the Emperor and in its spiritual aspects by the Pope. Most men still assumed that this pattern of feudal and ecclesiastical organization was God's design for Christendom. But the discrepancies between the form and the reality were growing at a bewildering pace. In parts of Europe—especially in North Italy, for example—economic and social power lay in fact with a class which had no place in the pattern, the "middle class" of merchants, industrialists, lawyers, and scholars. Political power rested in an institution unknown to the medieval pattern, the sovereign, territorial state. Within the busy, swarming cities of Italy there were careers wide open to talent—and hot competition to excel, whether as scholar or artist or professional soldier or political despot. Between the city-states there was a constant jockeying for territory and *Lebensraum*, a struggle for power untempered by any respect for higher authority of Pope or Emperor. Respect for legitimate authority, for what Burke would later call "precedent, prescription, and antiquity," was still dominant in much of Europe. But in Italy it yielded to admiration for talent and determination, inventiveness and virtuosity.

In other words, something like the modern sovereign, territorial state and something like modern capitalistic practice in commerce, industry, and even agriculture (in England, for instance) had appeared in the Europe of 1500. But there were no categories of thought through which these developments could be understood, let alone be controlled. The Middle Ages had an unshakable sense of right and justice, but never any very effective way of enforcing the right. There was always a principle to cover every incident, a law to apply to every case, but there were no effective sanctions. Here in early sixteenth century Europe were strong rulers and powerful merchants creating a kind of illegitimate order of their own. Was it enough simply to put them down as "tyrants" and "despots," "monopolists" and "usurers," using the traditional categories of thought? Was there no better way to understand them, no new perspective in which the strange new world of 1500 A.D. might become more intelligible?

Our twentieth century attitude in such a situation, I suppose, would be to say: "Get our economists and political scientists on the problem; hire a staff, apply for a foundation grant, and rent an electronic calculator; if the money holds out, we should have the answers in a few years." Fortunately or unfortunately, there were no such methods or resources available in the generation of Machiavelli and More. What *was* available was a new store of ancient political and social wisdom, and to this they turned with eagerness. Men began to reread Aristotle and Cicero, Thucydides and Polybius, Livy and Tacitus, with new purpose and understanding. Here was a literature concerned with politics and morals, with civil and foreign war, with tyranny and revolution, with justice and might—in other words, with every aspect of the struggle for power, among individuals within the state and among states themselves. To thoughtful fifteenth century readers all this was exciting—far more relevant than medieval chronicle or scholastic philosophy—and of course more practical than a "scientific method" which was still in its infancy. Their contemporary experience enabled them to understand the ancient writers, as schoolmen of two centuries earlier could not have done; and their reading in turn deepened their understanding of contemporary politics and diplomacy.

Modern political thought, in other words, resulted from the *coincidence* of rapid social change with the classical revival at the close of the Middle Ages. As new economic and political practices came into almost intolerable conflict with older habits of thought, a relatively untapped storehouse of social insight was discovered or rediscovered. *The Prince* and *Utopia* were not the only products of this fruitful coincidence, but they were perhaps the greatest.[1]

*   *   *

The peculiar blend of disillusioned realism and patriotic idealism which formed Machiavelli's character can be seen developing slowly during his early career as civil servant and diplomat. Reading his letters of these years with a view to tracing out this development can be a fascinating exercise.

In June 1498, a month after Savonarola's execution, Machiavelli got his first job with the republican government of Florence, and for the next fourteen years he served as Chancellor and Secretary to the ruling council of the city and as diplomatic envoy on numerous legations—to Paris, to the Emperor, to the Pope, to Cesare Borgia, and to many of the neighboring city-states. The picture we get of him during these years is that of an exceptionally acute observer of the political scene, unquestioningly faithful to his government although sometimes critical of its policies, always conscious of the weakness of the city-state he represents, always anxious to compensate by sheer intelligence for this weakness by turning up ingenious solutions to unsolvable problems, yet usually aware of the grim limits on Florentine freedom of action. He is generally second-in-command on any given legation, not first—which suggests that his bosses value his brains above his judgment. Occasionally he compares someone's policy with that of the Roman Republic in similar circumstances, to the advantage of the ancients, which suggests that although he is not a man of wide culture, he is reading the ancient historians.

His two constant preoccupations are the disunity at home and the weakness abroad that make his government's job the nightmare that it is. The Pazzi Conspiracy of 1478, that lurid plot to murder Lorenzo the Magnificent in church, had made a deep impression on him at the age of nine, and all his life he was to be concerned with the problem of *parte*, or factions, and their disintegrating effect on the State. But an even deeper impression had been left on him by the invasion of Italy in 1494 by Charles VIII of France, the invasion that first revealed the startling inferiority of a land of petty, warring city-states to a well-organized national monarchy. Five more times Italy was to be invaded before Machiavelli's government fell—once more by France, twice by the Emperor, and twice by Spain. The last attack by Spain in 1512 overthrew the republican regime in Florence and restored the Medici to power. In her weakness Florence had made an alliance with France, and, in a stubborn display of civic honor, she stuck by the alliance long after it was clear that Spain was going to beat France out for control of the Italian peninsula. In a parallel display of personal honor, Machiavelli's close friend and superior Piero Soderini refused to use unconstitutional means to save himself and his government in the crisis. In August 1512 Soderini fled. Some two months later Machiavelli was dismissed from office, and shortly after this a plot to destroy the new Medici rulers was discovered. Machiavelli's name was found on a list of those to be approached, and Machiavelli himself was imprisoned and tortured to reveal what he knew. Released in February 1513, he retired to a house of his in the country ten miles south of the city, where he had a tantalizing glimpse of the Duomo from his garden. And here he was left to put together the broken pieces of his life as well as he could, with a wife and four children to support, no job, and no visible prospects of getting one.

His letters during this crucial year 1513 to his friend Vettori (who was Florentine ambassador at Rome) and to Soderini (who had fled to Dalmatia) give fascinating glimpses of how a disappointed civil servant of a third-rate republic was led to become the first modern analyst of political power.[2] He was bored, frustrated, and resentful, worried about where the next meal was coming from, and acutely homesick for the world of politics and diplomacy which was his life's blood. He knew perfectly well that he was fitted for one career and one only. At forty-three he could not become a merchant or farmer overnight. "Fortune has so devised that since I cannot talk of the silk trade or the wool trade or of profit and loss, I have to talk of politics," he writes Vettori in April. "I have only one choice: either to talk of politics or to take a vow of silence." His mind runs restlessly over recent events—every state breaking treaties but Florence, every statesman forgetting the ordinary rules of morality but Soderini with his constitutional scruples. He has come to the conclusion, he writes Soderini, that the sole criterion of policies should be their *results*, not the means used to attain them. The same end can be attained by different means, just as you can get to the same place by different roads. "Just *why* different procedures should now help and now hinder, I do not know," he writes, "*but I would like to know.*" He thinks the answer is that "times and circumstances" change, and that the means suitable for one time are disastrous for another. Vettori asks him what he thinks of the latest move of Ferdinand, King of Spain. Isn't it foolish? Machiavelli jumps at the chance to put his rusting intellect to work and writes ten pages in reply. There is really no problem, he says, if you see that Ferdinand is not much of a statesman—just lucky. His letter will seem a jumble, he concludes apologetically, but he is in the country, never sees a human face (Machiavelli was always given to exaggeration), and knows "nothing of what is going on in the world." Later he argues that Vettori overrates Venetian power; the real danger to Italy comes from the Swiss and the French. "I don't know just what Aristotle says about countries that have been destroyed. What interests me more than theory is *what is, what has been, and what may reasonably happen.*"

Then in the most famous letter he ever wrote (December 10, 1513), Machiavelli tells Vettori how, when evening comes, he is in the habit of putting off his soiled clothes, putting on his court dress, and spending four hours of uninterrupted bliss in the company of his favorite classical authors. With them he partakes of that food which alone he can call his own and for which he was born, he says. He asks them questions, and they answer. Since Dante says there is no knowing apart from remembering, he has put down on paper some of the things he has learned from these older and wiser minds. "I have written a pamphlet which I am calling *On Principalities*. In it I go as deeply as I can into the subject, discussing the definition of monarchy, how many kinds of monarchies there are, and how they are won, held, and lost. . . . Any head of a state, and especially a new one, should find it interesting." He explains frankly that he is dedicating it to Giuliano de' Medici because he desperately needs a job and hopes the Medici will give him one. "Anybody, it seems to me, should be glad to have the services of a man who has acquired so much experience at the expense of other employers. Of my trustworthiness there could be no doubt. Having so long kept faith with people, I would not be likely to begin betraying now. A man who has kept his word loyally for forty-three years, as I have, could not change his nature very easily. The fact that I am a poor man is proof of my loyalty and honor." Four times the word *fede* (faith) occurs in these last sentences.[3] Obviously the writer is deeply concerned to impress even on his friend, who must know it, that patriotism and his pledged word come before party loyalty with him.

This then was the origin of *The Prince*. Perhaps it is evident from this account why those who have read the book over the years have argued—and still argue violently—over its purpose and meaning. Was it simply a cool, disillusioned analysis of how to get and hold on to power, with the last patriotic chapter added as a sort of afterthought to give the analysis some respectable use? Or did it, on the contrary, all lead up to the last chapter? Was it an honest and passionate appeal to the Medici to become the saviors of Italy from the foreign barbarians? Did the author really mean what he said about playing the beast rather than the man, seeming to have the private virtues but not being hampered by them, breaking faith if it was to your advantage? Was this the Machiavelli who was so proud of his own word once given and of his republic's reputation for good faith? Was he perhaps being satiric in *The Prince*, showing up despotism for what it really was so that all the people could take warning? Or was he even trying to trap the young Medici into following his precepts and thus getting themselves thrown out of Florence by an outraged populace, so that Machiavelli's republican party could get back in? Was he thoroughly immoral in what he said—or simply amoral —or was he sketching a new sort of morality—or was he beneath it all as thoroughly moral as any medieval schoolman, but simply disillusioned with the way things actually were in his day?[4]

There is no simple answer to these questions. All of these theories about the meaning of Machiavelli's *Prince* were broached before the sixteenth century came to a close, and all of them are in one way or another still alive today. A consensus of scholarly opinion today on the meaning of *The Prince*, however, might run somewhat as follows: Machiavelli wrote the book at white-hot speed in the fall of 1513. Into it went a good many disparate and even contradictory emotions and desires: resentment about his misfortune, disillusionment with legal and moral ways of doing things if this was where they landed you, desire to understand what had happened and how to avoid its happening again, desire to show off his political perspicacity to the new rulers of Florence in order to get his job back, a hope that out of writing some good would come—to him, to Florence, to Italy, perhaps even to posterity. In every chapter—in some more clearly than in others— he was trying to do two things at once: to understand and to reform. The two were related in a simple enough way: without understanding there could be no reform. The reason why reform schemes of intellectuals have invariably failed in the past, he is convinced, is that they have not been founded on politics as they actually *are*. He is perfectly aware that he is breaking with tradition, with the "Mirror of Princes" literature which urged princes to act like good men and assumed that everything would be all right if they did. "Since, however, it has been my intention to write something which may be of use to the understanding reader, it has seemed wiser to me to follow the real truth of the matter rather than what we imagine it to be," he says in Chapter 15. How we actually live is "so different from how we ought to live" that anyone who wants to seize and hold power must "learn how not to be good." It is all too easy to point out the flaw in the argument. If the goal is really "to set up a new state," enriching it and strengthening it with "good arms, good laws, good alliances, and good examples," as Chapter 24 seems to suggest— and this is estimating the goal at its best—will this end be achieved by the means suggested or will the means corrupt the end? Does obsession with the power factors involved in any political situation result in a regime adorned with "good laws" and "good examples," or does it result merely in irresponsible despotism and more corruption?

Machiavelli never really answered this question, but he was too intelligent to ignore it entirely. Whether by original design or not, *The Prince* became a sort of "Part I" to a larger work in Machiavelli's mind, a book on republics. Sometime between 1515 and 1517, when he began to visit his friends in the city once more and to discuss the classical historians with them in the Rucellai gardens, his *Discourses on Livy* took shape.[5] In this long and rambling work Machiavelli gave a more leisurely account of his political ideal and how it might be attained.

His historical ideal was the Roman Republic. The *Discourses* were concerned with the reason for Rome's greatness and (by implication) the rules for success which apply to any state. Machiavelli had discarded eternity and infinity as the criteria by which political success is to be judged, and had substituted duration in time and extension in space. Rome was great because her regime lasted so long and because her rule extended so widely.

The question was, what general rules for this kind of success could be discovered?

"I have decided to enter upon a new way, as yet untrodden by anyone else," Machiavelli writes at the beginning of the *Discourses*. This "new way," he explains, is the serious study of history with a view to developing a science of politics as a yardstick for social reform. Everyone reads and admires the ancients, he says, but no one *does* anything about his reading. The trouble is that men read history for fun when they ought to read it for profit. Machiavelli hopes that those who read his book will be able to draw "those practical lessons which one should seek to obtain from the study of history."

The "new way" echoes Polybius and is compressed (in I, 39) into one arresting paragraph, which merits quoting in full:

> If the present be compared with the remote past, it is easily seen that in all cities and in all peoples there are the same desires and the same passions as there always were. So that, if one examines with diligence the past, it is easy to foresee the future of any commonwealth, and to apply those remedies which were used of old; or if one does not find that remedies were used, to devise new ones owing to the similarity of events. But since such studies are neglected and what is read is not understood, or, if it is understood, is not applied in practice by those who rule, the consequence is that similar scandals occur at all times.

What Machiavelli seems to say here is that *because* human nature is always the same and *because* history goes round in cycles, knowledge and prediction are possible. But since the regular cyclical repetition seems to depend on men's *ignorance* of the process, knowledge of its rules and the proper "remedies" may somehow break the repetitive pattern and history may straighten out into progress in a straight line. Whether he meant to say this or not, I am not sure. What he did say quite clearly was that a careful study of history and of contemporary politics would reveal maxims and rules which would give the statesman both knowledge and control of the political process in any age, provided the proper adjustments were made to "times and circumstances."

Machiavelli's "new way" provided a new intellectual and moral framework in which to set the confusing political developments of his day. This new perspective might be set down somewhat summarily as follows:

The world in which we find ourselves is a treacherous, constantly changing affair. Whether it is ultimately an ordered cosmos we do not know, but it does not look as if it were. Man is alone in this world and on his own. Most men are ignorant, ambitious, ungrateful, and untrustworthy. Among individuals and groups there is a constant struggle for power. Human desires are limitless. If it is not ambition that drives men on to excess, it is fear. Democracies and republics are just as insatiable for power under certain circumstances as dictatorships and despotisms. There are no "safe" courses in diplomacy and politics, only choices between lesser evils and lesser dangers. In this world there are a few men—only a few—who have intelligence, courage, and public spirit. If these few will only exercise their brains and wills, and not be squeamish about the means they use, perhaps some limited good may be achieved, some stability gained in the midst of flux, some virtue in the midst of corruption. The best that they can do is to study the repetitive patterns of social existence as carefully as they can, decide upon the best courses, choose their ways with intelligence and boldness, and stick by their choices with determination.

Machiavelli saw the essentially demonic nature of power, as Gerhard Ritter remarks.[6] He saw that power is never tamed by moral precepts and that often the worst anarchy is the result of the best intentions. He never doubted the value of personal morality, as his own career proved, but he came to feel that there is a political morality which has its own autonomy and which must inevitably cancel out personal morality in moments of crisis. He was a ruthless critic of all who dreamed of ends without any concern for whether the means existed to attain them—and of all

who saw how to attain their ends but lacked the courage to act
on their insight. The new political morality which he sketched
out was thoroughly pragmatic, to be tested not by intentions but
by results. There was little if any continuity between this political
morality and the traditional personal morality of the classical and
Christian traditions. He found a "new way" as he hoped, but it
had too little continuity, too little organic relationship with the
old for healthy well-balanced growth. He saw two of the dimensions of power, the physical and the intellectual, and perhaps he
tended to exaggerate both. Exaggeration of the power of the pen
is par-for-the-course with intellectuals in general. But exaggerat-
ing the power of the sword is what happens when intellectuals
lean over backward to prove that they are tough-minded men of
affairs. ("Scholars and literary men often seem more given to the
inverted idealism of *Realpolitik* than working diplomats," Garrett
Mattingly observes.)[7] But in a sense Machiavelli missed the third
dimension of power, the moral dimension. At least it is possible
to argue that Machiavelli, the consummate realist, the resolute
facer of things-as-they-are, had one blind spot, an inability to see
the reality of moral and spiritual forces in the lives of men.

*   *   *

Some five years after Machiavelli's death, a close student of his
little book on *The Prince*, Thomas Cromwell, became the chief
minister of King Henry VIII of England. His only rival for the
King's favor, Sir Thomas More, had resigned as Lord Chancellor
the day after the clergy acknowledged Henry as Supreme Head
of the Church of England in place of the Pope (May 1532).
Cromwell brought More a message from the King soon after his
resignation, and they had a lengthy talk. At the end, More said:
"Master Cromwell, you are now entered into the service of a
most noble, wise, and liberal prince; if you will follow my poor
advice, you shall, in your counsel-giving unto his Grace, ever tell
him what he *ought* to do, but never what he is *able* to do . . . For
if a lion knew his own strength, hard were it for any man to rule

him." More's biographer remarks that we can think of this inter-
view "as one where the Utopian faced the Machiavellian, provided we use these words without prejudice . . . It was not
necessarily idealism facing villainy."⁸ Whatever it was, the wider
issues behind this encounter—moralism vs. realism—what ought
to be vs. what is—have fascinated later students all the way from
Jean Bodin in the later sixteenth century to Gerhard Ritter in the
twentieth.

As we have remarked already, some of the differences between
The Prince and *Utopia* are the result quite simply of the differences
between Machiavelli's Italy and More's England. The underlying
problems were the same: the decay of medieval institutions, the
growth of strong centers of political power, and the spread of
capitalistic practices in the economy. But there was more continuity with the immediate past in More's England, and the social
tensions resulting from change took different forms. Henry VII,
the first Tudor, had pretty well scotched the danger of feudal
anarchy by strengthening the monarchy, building up a surplus in
the treasury, holding a tight rein on the nobility, and keeping
England out of war abroad. His methods were not always scrupulous, but since the end result was peace and order and surcease of
civil war, Machiavelli would have approved—and so have most
modern historians. A sensitive contemporary like Thomas More,
however, might well have been dismayed by Henry's financial
exactions, his enforcement of long-forgotten laws to raise money,
and his apparent practice of getting a grant from Parliament for
a war, then calling off the war and keeping the money. The same
kind of observer might well have been disturbed for different
reasons by the adventurous foreign policy of his son, Henry VIII.
Within five years of coming to the throne in 1509, Henry VIII
had squandered his father's surplus on a futile war with France,
the chief motive of which was to gain glory for the young
monarch.

Machiavelli had been impressed by two things as he was growing to maturity: the factional fights which tore his native city to

pieces, and its weakness with respect to the great powers of the day. Thomas More, on the other hand, was a subject of one of the better-run national monarchies of the sixteenth century. His country had just come through a time of troubles but was now strong, united, and in no real danger of invasion or conquest. In fact, if there was any danger, it was that England would let her recovery go to her head and would dissipate her new-found strength in continental adventures. There was little danger any more of organized feudal revolt or lawlessness. But there were signs that the energies of the ruling class, which had once gone into the wars with France and the Wars of the Roses, were now going into economic exploitation of the people and cut-throat competition for favor at the court. More was the son of a London lawyer, and he spent some years in his teens as a page in the household of Cardinal Morton, a churchman of integrity and devotion. It was natural for him to look at the social problems of his day through the eyes of a city-dweller or of a clergyman. The danger, as he saw it, was not so much anarchy as tyranny, not so much urban factions as feudal greed and arrogance, not so much national weakness as national aggressiveness.

The intellectual influence of overwhelming importance on More was Christian Humanism. It is hard today to recapture the enthusiasm of the Christian Humanists—Reuchlin, Erasmus, Lefèvre d'Étaples, John Colet, and More himself—because what they believed possible seems utterly unrealistic as we look back on it. They believed they could save their society by reviving the best in both classical and Christian antiquity, going back to Plato and the Gospels, reconciling the two traditions, and stripping off all medieval accretions and distortions. They were Christian intellectuals with an infectious belief in the power of good scholarship and proper education. They thought that if men only *knew* what Socrates said and what Jesus preached, if men could only be made to see the gulf between apostolic Christianity and sixteenth century Christianity, reform would inevitably follow. No one could stop it, they believed, once men of intelligence and good will had been exposed to the best that had come down from ancient Greece and Palestine.

Practically all of these Christian Humanists were pure intellectuals—writers, teachers, scholars—idealists with no professional responsibility for carrying into practice the reforms they advocated. Thomas More was the outstanding exception: a deeply devoted Christian and a scholar, but one who was called early to a busy and exhausting career as a lawyer and public official. Henry VIII and Wolsey came to know the young More and covet his services for the crown. Just when the King began actually to press him to enter the royal service we do not know, but we find him a member of an embassy to the Netherlands in the summer of 1515, still merely representing the City of London's interests on an *ad hoc* mission and not yet a royal official.

This embassy proved to be an important event in More's life. Apparently there were lulls in the negotiations (as there always are) while both sides waited for further instructions from home. More visited an old friend, Peter Giles, in Antwerp, and there was time for talk, for thought, and for writing. Somehow, away from his family, away from his native land, temporarily unoccupied by the press of business, he began to let his imagination take flight. The world was surely in a parlous state, as perhaps it always had been. More had seen its seamy side as a lawyer. He was a good lawyer, but hated most of what he had to do. He was peculiarly sensitive to what happens to the little man in the toils of the law and the clutches of the rich. He was convinced that the economic revolution which had struck England—the conversion of arable land to pasture because of the profit to be made from sheep-farming—was causing misery and suffering among the poor. Unemployment led to vagabondage, vagabondage to thievery, then the thieves were punished by a savage death penalty—which did not stop the thievery or save the souls of the victims. Meanwhile the rich squandered the profits of their exploitation and monopoly on clothes, servants, and luxuries. Everywhere pride, greed, and idleness—and among princes, nothing but a ceaseless and senseless struggle for more gold and more territory.

Not a pretty picture—and surely an excuse for cynicism. But to a Christian Humanist there were certain unexploited resources in the classical and Christian traditions which might be utilized to help solve sixteenth century problems, if only they could be brought vividly before men's imaginations. This matter of "mine-and-thine," for instance, which was at the root of all the trouble: Plato knew that if his governors were to develop any true sense of community among themselves, private property must be denied them. The first apostles held all their goods in common, and the first rule of all truly strenuous Christian communities ever since had been renunciation of property. Granted that man will always remain a sinner. Still, his nature is to a large extent the product of his environment. What if he should take seriously the ideals of Plato's Republic and the medieval monastery? Wasn't it theoretically possible to build a society based on communism of goods in which pride in its way of life and satisfaction with the results would curb the natural tendency to greed of its individual members? Perhaps such a society actually existed, now, somewhere in the vast expanses of the world recently opened up to wondering European eyes since Columbus's momentous voyage twenty-three years before. At any rate, the startling tales of mariners back from the New World and walking the streets of Antwerp suggested that this sort of thing was not beyond believing.

This is a not altogether fanciful account of what went through More's head in the summer of 1515 as he whiled away the time at Peter Giles's in Antwerp. It is based, of course, on what came out of his head later. At the end of the summer, More had finished a manuscript describing the people and customs of "Utopia." It probably represented Book II of what we have in print today plus the first five pages of Book I as preface.[9] It was a startlingly original combination of imagination and hard realism, lightened by turns of sheer wit and horseplay. Almost every feature of Utopian life and thought (except the more obviously humorous bits) was designed as a remedy or palliative to some concrete social evil which More knew at first hand. His realistic lawyer's grasp of his own society, its economic, social, and political problems, lay behind every flight of the imagination. He drew on his wide knowledge of classical and Christian literature for ideas, but there was no literal copying of tradition anywhere. For instance, communism in Utopia is the way of life of the whole nation, not of a few governors (as in Plato) or of an isolated group (as in the monastery); yet there is still much of Plato's and St. Benedict's spirit in it.

The second book of *Utopia* is a Christian Humanist's carefully developed remedy for the three key sins of English society— sloth, greed, and especially pride—as the brilliant little study of J. H. Hexter shows convincingly.[10] Everyone is compelled to work in Utopia so that idleness may never become a badge of social privilege. Greed is nipped in the bud by providing everyone with economic security. And pride is given nothing to feed upon, at least in the individual's life. With true Christian insight, More rates pride as a deadlier sin than greed—"the princess and mother of all mischief," in fact. Without pride, without the limitless desire to outshine other persons, to show off, to outspend and outconsume all social rivals, to play God on earth, greed would be comparatively easy to handle, More seems to suggest. At any rate, the strict and dreary egalitarianism of Utopia is designed just as clearly to exterminate pride as it is to curb avarice.

More's intent was serious: to show how an ideal society based on reason alone without the benefit of revelation might still put to shame a Christian society which did not live up to the truth revealed to it. The literalist can of course walk heavy-footedly through *Utopia* and demonstrate that More did not mean this or that seriously, and the pedant can prove that it is all a story told by an old traveler and that More never said *he* believed it. But there is too much in both the design and detail of *Utopia* that has the ring of passionate sincerity about it for any thoughtful reader to doubt that the writer was serious. What did More mean to accomplish by picturing an imaginary island, remarkably like England in geography and remarkably unlike England in social customs, supposedly in actual existence here and now, and removed from Europe not in time but simply by space? I think he was trying to say: stretch your imaginations, exercise your fancy, get out of the mental ruts men have been in for centuries, stop reconciling yourselves to social evil as inevitable, and keep steadily before you the picture of *what might be* as the measure of what is. You may not, and probably will not, set up communism of goods overnight, he seems to say, but if you have seriously considered the advantages of a communist society, at least you will never again look on private property as an absolute, an untouchable right, to be defended against all attempts to limit it.

Parts of *Utopia*, it has been remarked before this, read like a commentary on a book that More had never read, *The Prince*. Machiavelli never forgets what is "good," what "ought to be" from the standpoint of personal morality, but he insists on a clearcut distinction between this and what is "good" in public policy. The prince should "stick to the path of good" so far as he is able, "but if the necessity arises he should know how to follow evil." Rulers who think little of breaking their word have generally won out in recent experience over those who are more scrupulous. "Hence a wise leader cannot and should not keep his word when keeping it is not to his advantage." "Everyone sees what you seem to be, few experience what you really are," Machiavelli concluded; "the end is all that counts." "Let a prince then concern himself with the acquisition or the maintenance of a state; the means employed will always be considered honorable and praised by all, for the mass of mankind is always swayed by appearances and by the outcome of an enterprise. And in the world there is only the mass . . . ."[11] The narrator of *Utopia*, Raphael Hythlodaye, remarks with obvious irony that agreements between princes are strictly observed in Europe, of course, but in the countries near Utopia princes find loopholes in treaties by crafty dodges which they would loudly condemn if used in private dealings. The Utopians therefore see that there are "two kinds of justice, one the people's justice, mean, lowly, bound by fetters on every side, so that it cannot jump the fences, the other the justice of princes, which is more majestic and so much freer than the other that it may take whatever it wants." The Utopians disdain to follow this "justice of princes." They will not divorce their public policy from principles of private morality. They make no formal alliances whatever, in the belief that "men are bound more adequately by good will than by pacts, more strongly by their hearts than by their words."[12]

The chief difference between Machiavelli's thought-world and that of More, however, cannot be illustrated by direct quotation. It has to do with time and change. Utopia is a completely static society. Since its foundation by King Utopus there has been no significant change, no development, no "history" in fact, and presumably there will be no change in the future. The assumptions underlying Utopia are: first, evil is essentially social in origin and so any effective attack on it must be through the creation of a new social structure, a new environment; second, this environment, once it is created, will curb and control individual tendencies to evil, even if it will not entirely root out individual wrongdoing; and third, there are timeless rules of reason which can be discovered and used in designing this new social structure. With much of this Machiavelli, especially in the *Discourses*, would agree. But Machiavelli could never escape from the time dimension as the Utopians succeed in doing. His test of a prince's *virtù* was ability to change with "times and circumstances," his test of a republic was ability to endure in time and expand in space. Nothing is at rest in *The Prince* and the *Discourses;* everything is at rest in *Utopia*. To Machiavelli the real world is a continuous struggle for power between competing vitalities; to More, in *Utopia*, it is a world in which power can be controlled and disciplined, nay, even rendered harmless. Machiavelli is consciously revolutionary, always striving for a "new method," a "new way." More is a conservative who pictures a society built on reason devoting an enormous part of its energy simply to preserving the status quo.

This last is worth examining more closely. Utopia is an artificial island—it was King Utopus who dug the fifteen-mile channel that separates it from the continent. Geographical isolation both makes possible and intensifies the Utopians' psychological isolation from their neighbors. What holds the rather loose federation of Utopian cities together is what we would call national sentiment—pride in the Utopian way of life, which they are persuaded is the best in the world until God reveals a better to them.[13] There are all kinds of ingenious devices to preserve the status quo, to keep the number in each family constant, to keep the population at a constant level, to balance trade, and to maintain international peace so that the Utopian welfare state may not be disturbed in its enjoyment of the good life. The Utopians are far more wealthy and powerful than any of their neighbors, and so they go to war only in "just" causes. The list of "just" causes, however, is rather long. It includes resistance to Utopian colonization of backward areas and injuries done to merchants of allied powers. The Utopians use their overwhelming power only to execute right and justice—and in Raphael's account of it, at least, their neighbors seem to grant that the Utopians' moral and cultural superiority justifies their foreign policy. There is a strong streak of moral righteousness in all that they do. They are harder on their own condemned criminals than on their foreign slaves because the former turned to crime "in spite of their excellent education and moral training." Their one objective in going to war is "to accomplish what they would gladly have achieved without war if just terms had been granted in time." Because Utopian manhood is so precious, they prefer to fight by the crafty use of money and propaganda, and by tricks which would delight a Machiavellian. They use their friends' and allies' troops before their own. But if they are finally forced to fight, they fight hard, knowing they are in the right, and they impose stiff indemnities on their defeated victims.[14]

More was thoroughly medieval in his belief in timeless standards of right and justice, as Gerhard Ritter points out.[15] He thought that the use of power was justified only as a means of enforcing right or justice, and that war made sense only as an instrument of justice meting out punishment—not as a more or less natural result of competing wills-to-live, as it seemed to Machiavelli. More believed that power could be harnessed and tamed by righteousness. But perhaps his later German critics are justified in asking how those neighboring backward peoples would really feel about the high-and-mighty Utopians, with their gold which they never enjoy, their "dumping" policy in foreign trade, their big citizen army, and their high moral principles. Is the struggle for power abolished by imagining it out of existence? Or does it slip in by the back door after the moralist has bolted and barred the front? More's *Utopia* is the work of a conscientious Christian Humanist, humane and civilized in spirit. But there is a curious streak of moralism and self-righteousness in it that is not unrelated to the later More who conscientiously supported the burning of heretics.

*   *   *

Sometimes when I am musing about the apparently unbridgeable gulf between the thought-worlds of Machiavelli and Thomas More, I fall into a kind of daydream. In the dream I discover a hitherto unknown manuscript in a sixteenth century hand entitled "Further remarks by Raphael Hythlodaye after his conversations with Sir Thomas More at Antwerp." In it Raphael tells of his astonishment at discovering only two days before that there was someone else in Antwerp who had been in Utopia. Raphael had lost no time in looking this person up and had found him to be an Italian *condottiere* who had risen from obscurity through his military profession to be despot of one of the wealthier North Italian cities. Although he had displayed considerable political virtuosity in the job, he had finally been driven into exile after a bloody uprising and had somehow shipped out to the New World

to recoup his fortunes. He had been shipwrecked on Utopia shortly after Raphael's departure and had spent almost six months on or
near the island before returning to Europe. At first he was re-
luctant to recall his experiences to mind, but as Raphael won his
confidence, the whole story gradually came out.

As soon as he had recovered from the experience of shipwreck,
the Prince (Raphael never referred to him in any other way) had
been struck by the prosperity, the contentment, and the civic
virtue of the Utopians. Here was a really stable and secure society,
he thought, unlike any city-state in the maelstrom of contemporary Italy. In fact, in its citizens' civic virtue, their pride in their
way of life, their regard for their own elected governors, their
military preparedness, and the healthy respect they inspired in
neighboring countries, Utopia resembled the Roman Republic
more closely than any contemporary state the Prince could think
of. Here was a country worth governing, he thought, a prize
worth grasping—if it could be grasped.

He told Raphael that during his first few weeks in Utopia he
amused himself by trying to analyze the power-structure of the
society. Did the Syphograuntes, the Tranibores, and the elected
prince hold the people in subjection by love or by fear? What
were the factions in the council chamber and what was the balance
of power among them? Did the government rest ultimately upon
popular support, upon the favor of the nobles, or upon control
of the military? Did the laws protect the property, the lives, and
the wives of the citizens? Was there a citizen army, and was it
strong enough to protect the island against any possible combination of enemies? These were the questions any man of intelligence
and experience would ask about any state, he was sure, but the
Prince became increasingly baffled and bewildered in his search
for answers. None of the answers he knew seemed to fit. The
elected officials seemed to wield very little power of any sort.
There were no issues of any importance debated in the council
chamber, no intrigues, no factions. There were no nobles and no
professional soldiers, so the government obviously rested on the

people for support. But since there was no class in society *against* whom the people supported the government, this support was a vague and shadowy thing. The laws did not protect the citizens' property for the simple reason that there was no property. There seemed to be no need to protect the lives and wives of the people by stringent legislation because crimes of lust and violence were remarkably few. There was a citizen army, the Prince was happy to note, and it was the most effective military force in that part of the world. But who controlled it or determined when it was to be used was not altogether clear. All in all, it was a frustrating inquiry.

The Prince was sure, however, that beneath the baffling surface of calm and contentment there were stresses and strains, contending forces, and ambitious individuals as there always are everywhere. He set out to find them and then to make use of them, as he had done all his life. For a time he thought he had a group of Syphograuntes interested in overthrowing the ruler and setting up a popular despotism under himself—until they suddenly realized what his scheme really amounted to and, in a grave but kindly way, explained to him that there was no point in it. The Prince realized with astonishment that these were men utterly without ambition, either for power or wealth, shamefully uninterested in bettering their families' position in the social scale or leaving a name for themselves in the historical record. He turned with impatience to the slaves, got the confidence of a fairly sizeable group of them, and thought he had the makings of a first-rate rebellion—until he discovered that the war prisoners among them considered their present lot better than anything they had known in their old countries, while most of the native Utopians considered their enslavement a perfectly fair punishment for the crimes they had committed—far preferable at least to capital punishment.

In disgust the Prince crossed the narrow channel separating Utopia from the mainland and began to nose around among the Utopians' neighbors. Here he found people and politics that were more familiar to him. There was considerable resentment about Utopian economic policy, fear of their gold, and dislike of their toplofty attitude to less fortunate peoples. Within a few weeks the Prince had a formidable and (as he thought) firm alliance settled between nearly all the nations within striking distance of Utopia. The public treaty mentioned only "defence against the communist imperialists," but a secret clause pledged each signatory to support an invasion set for two months ahead. For several weeks things looked good for the Prince. Then reports began to trickle in which indicated that the Utopians had friends on the mainland, persons who believed in the righteousness of their cause and the superiority of their social system. Money was being spent surreptitiously in large sums to corrupt leaders of the coalition, and vague rumors of changes of heart began to circulate. The feeling grew in some quarters that perhaps it was better to remain satellite states under the mild and generally beneficent rule of Utopia than to risk international anarchy among themselves, or possibly submission to the Zapoletes, those brutal mercenaries from the mountains, who might not go home after a war.

In this crisis the Prince showed all the *virtù* that a man of his character and experience would be expected to show. He made a fearful example of some of the waverers by skewering them to their chairs at a dinner party in his own house, on the principle that necessary frightfulness should be done all at once. He picked and trained his military units with care, on the principle that the sinews of war are not gold, but good soldiers. He held the tottering alliance together against the righteousness propaganda of the Utopians by constantly promising more and more of the Utopians' territory to each ally. And he saw that the Utopians were plied with propaganda to the effect that if they would surrender, the cooperative farms and dining halls would be broken up, the land given out to the individual farmers, and everyone allowed to throw away those drab uniform garments and wear what he liked. On the appointed day the invasion fleet sailed, with the triumphant Prince on the poop of the largest vessel, and a shout went up from the fleet as the men caught sight of the disciplined ranks of the Utopians drawn up along the shore, calm and untroubled because they knew they were in the right. . . .

But there the manuscript in my dream always breaks off short. What happened? Did the Prince win? Did he take over Utopia, as he had taken over his city in Italy? Or did the Utopians win and benevolently make him a slave, with a view to reforming his character? I do not know.

The fact is, I suppose, that the forces of the Machiavellian are forever about to overwhelm the forces of moralism, and the Utopians are forever standing imperturbable, ready to annihilate the forces of *Realpolitik* the moment they attack. The antinomy of realism and moralism in the analysis of politics must be argued through for each new generation, in the light of its particular historical circumstances and needs. In their day Machiavelli and More seemed utterly irreconcilable. To Machiavelli the ceaseless struggle for power must be accepted as one of the brute facts of life. You can learn how to use it, he seems to say, and in certain ideal circumstances you can balance power against power and so attain a certain stability and order; but you can never tame power, never outlaw it or ignore it. To Thomas More, in *Utopia*, on the other hand, the struggle for power may be so curbed and contained by the proper structure of law and right that for all practical purposes its potential for evil can be ignored forever. "I am glad," Raphael concludes his account, "that the Utopians have achieved their social organization, which I wish all mankind would imitate. Their institutions give their commonwealth a moral and social foundation for living happy lives, and as far as man can predict, these institutions will last forever. . . . As long as they maintain sound institutions and domestic harmony, they can never be overcome by the envious rulers near by, who have often attempted their ruin in vain."[16] The Machiavellian and the Utopian are thus symbols of an eternal contradiction. The Machiavellian sees only material power and is blind to moral and spiritual forces, the Utopian overestimates moral forces and thinks he can exorcise the demon of power in the end.

Machiavelli and More are not so impossibly far apart, however, as might appear at first. In fact, Felix Gilbert goes so far as to say that in its own time and place the foreign policy which Machiavelli advocated was so revolutionary as to be "utopian." Garrett Mattingly suggests that some of Machiavelli's most shocking advice to princes was basically satirical in intent, designed to show up unscrupulous rulers for what they were.[17] And it can easily be argued that the really important thing about *Utopia* in its own day was not its moralism and idealism, which had long histories, but its realistic grasp of contemporary social problems in their secular setting, which was new. As we have remarked already, Machiavelli was idealist as well as realist, and More was realist as well as idealist. The exact proportion of each will never be determined so long as students differ as widely as they do on the meaning of *The Prince* and *Utopia*.

The argument between realism and moralism in the conduct of public policy continues down to our own day in our own land. It is perhaps not surprising to see it articulated with particular clarity in the United States in the mid-twentieth century. We have been a people with a long isolationist tradition and strong moral beliefs, like the Utopians, but within two short generations we have been shocked out of our complacency by being thrust into a deadly competition for existence with a ruthless power of equal strength—in other words, into the world of Machiavelli. We have learned to act like Machiavelli's Prince—without losing our moral principles—and our public conscience is troubled. The two most eloquent spokesmen of realism and moralism in the conduct of our foreign policy, it seems to me, would be Mr. George Kennan, former ambassador to Moscow, and the late Mr. John Foster Dulles. I am not at all sure that Mr. Kennan would relish being compared with Machiavelli, and I think Mr. Dulles would definitely resent being likened to the papist, Thomas More. But there are amusing parallels nonetheless.

In the books and articles which each of them wrote around midcentury—books which were written like those we have been considering, rapidly and urgently, to inform the general reader and to reform public policy—the issue was once more argued with an eloquence almost worthy of their Renaissance predecessors.[18] To Kennan, the most serious fault in twentieth century American foreign policy has been "the legalistic-moralistic approach to international problems." Americans tend too easily to self-righteousness and moral superiority in their dealings with other powers. "This is a hard and cruel world we live in," he assumes. "We cannot, when it comes to dealings between governments, assign to moral values the same significance we give them in personal life." We can observe moral *methods* in our diplomacy—and Kennan is too good a Utopian to wish us to do anything else—but personal morality can never be a valid test of the *purposes* of a state, nor "a criterion for measuring and comparing the behavior of different states." It is better, he argues in Machiavellian vein but with Christian presuppositions, to accept the fact that we are a great power which has to do some of the things great powers have always had to do to survive, rather than to try constantly to appear morally superior to other nations. The worst wars are wars for righteousness, for unconditional surrender, not those for limited and concrete objectives. To John Foster Dulles, the real issues were moral issues. Where Kennan tended to emphasize the threat from Russia, the world power, Dulles tended to emphasize the threat from Communist ideology. "Moral judgment and world opinion" must be reckoned along with military power among the forces "which determine what men do and the intensity with which they do it." The United States rose to world power through her moral and spiritual qualities, he felt—not because of her isolation and the protection of the British navy, as a French critic slyly observed. We are engaged in a battle of creeds, not merely a conflict of world powers, and so Mr. Dulles would have us fight by spiritual revival at home and propaganda abroad before we draw the sword (like the

Utopians). He was never blind to the power factors in the situation confronting Americans, but he had great faith in legal structures and moral arguments, and like the Utopians he was never in doubt about who was right and who was wrong. One has the feeling that to Mr. Dulles the only excuse for going to war was that it was a war for righteousness.[19]

To the historian it seems clear that in this long argument between Machiavellians and Utopians the case is not one of contradiction but of complementarity. Machiavelli was right in insisting that no government which ignores the pure power factors in its position will survive long. And More, following the medieval tradition, was right in maintaining that positions of power must somehow be converted into structures of right if men are to give them their enduring support. Pascal, who was no political thinker, nevertheless summed it up in that bitter, penetrating way he had of stabbing to the heart of the matter in a few sentences:

> Justice without might is helpless; might without justice is tyrannical... We must therefore combine justice and might, and for this end make what is just strong, or what is strong just... Being unable to cause might to obey justice, men have made it just to obey might. Unable to strengthen justice, they have justified might.[20]

The irony was Machiavelli's, but the underlying faith was More's.

NOTES

1. In quoting from *The Prince* I have generally followed the new translation of T. G. Bergin (New York, Crofts Classics, 1947). In quoting from *Utopia* I have usually followed that of H. V. S. Ogden (New York, Crofts Classics, 1949).

2. In what follows, I have used the translations in *The Living Thoughts of Machiavelli*, ed. C. Sforza (London, 1942).

3. See J. H. Whitfield, *Machiavelli* (Oxford, 1947), p. 61.

4. See, e.g., Whitfield, Chaps. I, IV; A. H. Gilbert, *Machiavelli's Prince and its Forerunners* (Durham, 1938); F. Gilbert, "The Humanist Concept of the Prince and the *Prince of Machiavelli*," *Journal of Modern History*, XI (December 1939), 449-483, and "The Concept of Nationalism in Machiavelli's *Prince*," *Studies in the Renaissance, Publications of the Renaissance Society of America*, I, (1954), 38-48.

5. See *The Discourses of Niccolò Machiavelli*, ed. L. J. Walker, 2 vols. (New Haven, 1950); F. Gilbert, "The Composition and Structure of Machiavelli's *Discorsi*," *Journal*

of the History of Ideas, XIV (January 1953), 136-156; J. H. Hexter, "Seyssel, Machiavelli, and Polybius vi: the Mystery of the Missing Translation," *Studies in the Renaissance,* III (1956), 75-96; and H. Baron, "The *Principe* and the Puzzle of the Date of the *Discorsi,*" *Bibliothèque d'humanisme et renaissance,* XVIII (September 1956), 405-428. In what follows, I have used Walker's translation in quoting from the *Discourses.*

6. G. Ritter, *Machtstaat und Utopie* (1940); trans. as *The Corrupting Influence of Power* (Hadleigh, Essex, 1952).

7. In *Renaissance Diplomacy* (London, 1955), p. 40.

8. R. W. Chambers, *Thomas More* (New York, 1935), p. 291.

9. J. H. Hexter, *More's Utopia: the Biography of an Idea* (Princeton, 1952), pp. 26-29, *et passim.*

10. *Ibid.,* pp. 72-81.

11. *The Prince,* ch. 18.

12. *Utopia* (Crofts), pp. 62-63.

13. *Ibid.,* p. 79.

14. *Ibid.,* pp. 57, 63-70.

15. Ritter, *Corrupting Influence,* pp. 80 ff.

16. *Utopia,* p. 82.

17. F. Gilbert, in *Studies in the Renaissance,* I, 48; Mattingly, *Renaissance Diplomacy,* p. 166.

18. G. F. Kennan, *American Diplomacy, 1900-1950* (Chicago, 1951) and *Realities of American Foreign Policy* (Princeton, 1954) (particularly Chap. 2); J. F. Dulles, *War or Peace?* (New York, 1950). See also L. Brandt-Peltier, *Conceptions americaines de politique étrangère: Kennan-Dulles* (Geneva, 1953).

19. See especially Kennan, *American Diplomacy,* pp. 95 ff., *Realities . . . ,* pp. 47-50, 61; Dulles, pp. 16, 19; Brandt-Peltier, pp. 179-182.

20. *Pensées,* Everyman (1931), Nos. 298, 300.

MYRON P. GILMORE ∾ *The Renaissance Conception of the Lessons of History*

 NE OF THE KEYS TO THE UNDERSTANDING OF THE mentality of a past epoch is to be found in the study of its ideas about history. What men think about the past tells us also a good deal of what they think about the present. Perhaps the most important distinction between primitive and civilized societies is that in the former the memory of events in earlier generations is not differentiated, while in the latter a sense of the past adds a dimension to present existence. A man may react first of all to the similarities and even uniformities which unite his experience to that of his ancestors, or, on the other hand, he may be most impressed by the contrast between his and his great-grandfather's situation, but in either case he transcends his own immediate environment; in Becker's phrase, he enlarges his "specious present."[1] Whether he looks at change or continuity, the result of considering the past is in some sense a lesson of history. The effort to understand the past may fluctuate between the search for uniformities and the appreciation of the unique, but in either case history is an educative process in the literal sense of leading a man out of himself. It provides an enlargement of the horizon and discloses an infinite variety of views. Decisions about what part of the landscape to study and how to

study it are conditioned not only by the personality of the observer but more subtly by the civilization, period, generation, or social group to which he belongs.

It is obvious that different civilizations have entertained very different ideas of time and the historical process. The historical works of any epoch are in fact as much conditioned by the general "style" of the period in which they are produced as the creations of architecture, sculpture and painting. We are all familiar—perhaps too familiar—with the contrasts between oriental and occidental conceptions of time and, within western history, between the Greek idea of recurrence and the Hebrew idea of linear development. The Greeks, it is said, knew phenomena which had a beginning and an end and also those which had no beginning and no end, but they had no conception either of an act of creation which brought a universe into existence or of an absolutely unique event occupying the place of the incarnation in Christian history. We find another familiar example of the differences between modes of historical interpretation in the contrast between the medieval providential view of history and the doctrine of progress which was elaborated in the eighteenth century and has flourished until the shocks of the twentieth. These are illustrations on the most comprehensive scale but, even with the "sub-periods" in the history of modern western civilization, changes in the conception of the meaning of history have been characteristic of the successive stages in the intellectual development of Europe.

In periods of stability and peace history recedes into a distant background. In Victorian England history was generally considered to have stopped at the Battle of Waterloo in 1815, but in the twentieth century it is a usual feeling that we are only too much caught up in the historical process. By the traditional division that still prevails in most European countries *histoire moderne* commences with the Renaissance or Reformation and finishes with 1789 whereas *histoire contemporaine* still begins with the French Revolution. The estimates of what constitutes "history" as opposed to "present" have fluctuated with the even more varied value judgments on the relationship of past to present. From the time of the Greeks there have been some generations who have turned back to a golden age in the past and endowed a primitive society with all the virtues and none of the vices of civilization.[2] Others, however, have looked on primitive society as one in which all life was in Hobbes' famous phrase, "solitary, poor, nasty, brutish, and short." Some philosophers in the nineteenth century regarded their own age as the culmination of the historical process while others measured their own times against an idealized period in the past, the great age of Greece, or the thirteenth "greatest of centuries" and found in the comparison only grounds for despair.

These contrasts, between progress and decadence, between evolution and recurrence, between optimism and pessimism, have fixed the bounds within which the western tradition has elaborated its ideas on the meaning of history. In this long and complex evolution a significant stage is marked by the period of the Renaissance in which there appeared a new and distinctive attitude towards historical studies.

The concept of the Renaissance has given rise to much controversy and a voluminous literature.[3] The metaphor was originally invoked to describe certain intellectual and artistic achievements first in Italy and subsequently in the rest of Europe in the period from the fourteenth to the seventeenth century but modern usage has popularized its application to the period as a whole. In spite of the vague and multiple meanings which the term has in consequence acquired, it has become deeply embedded in our historical vocabulary. In general it is applied with more precision to intellectual rather than to institutional history, using the term intellectual in its broadest sense, and this is the more justifiable because the great changes of the period were in the realm of the arts and the mind and not in political and economic life.[4] The latter was far from static but, viewing the European scene as a whole, it cannot be said that the Renaissance saw transformations in institutions which matched in anything like the same degree those in the history of ideas. The intellectual revolution was profound, and was both cause and consequence of the enormous extension of knowledge and experience in time and space. Greek and Roman history and especially the latter came into ever clearer view and the increasing knowledge of classical civilization posed anew the problem of the relationship between classical and Christian values. The mass of information brought back to Europe by travellers and missionaries in the sixteenth century created an analogous problem on the relationship of contemporary non-Christian civilizations to that of western Europe. The exploration of antiquity preceded the exploration of Asia and the new world, and it is in fourteenth century Italy that we find the first consciously held new attitudes towards the classical past. In the elaboration of these attitudes as in so many other areas Petrarch was a figure of commanding importance and any description of the historical ideas of the Italian Renaissance must begin with a consideration of his thought.

In many of his works Petrarch reveals a preoccupation with time and the position of his own age in relation to the past and to the future. This is perhaps most dramatically apparent in the series of letters addressed to ancient authors in the last book of the *Familiares*. In these compositions Petrarch wrote to his favorite literary heroes in antiquity in the tone he would use in writing to his friends in his own age. It was an imaginative effort to cross the centuries which separated the classical authors from Petrarch but it was predicated on a real apprehension of the remoteness of the ancient world. The intensity of the longing together with the realization of the impossibility of its fulfilment created the conditions for these extraordinary communications.

In the letter to Livy Petrarch begins with the wish that he had been born in Livy's age or Livy in his. They would have been able to console each other. Petrarch bewails the destruction of the lost books and says that he resorts to reading Livy whenever he wishes to forget the conditions of Italy and the moral standards of his own time. "I am filled with bitter indignation," he writes, "against the mores of today when men value nothing except gold and silver and desire nothing except sensual pleasures." He is grateful to Livy for permitting him to forget the present evils and, as if closing a conversation which he had really had but which he can never have again, he concludes with the apostrophe: "Farewell forever, O matchless historian!" The letter is significantly dated, "Written in the land of the living, in that part of Italy and in that city in which I am now living and where you were once born and buried, in the vestibule of the temple of Justina Virge and in view of your very tombstone on the twenty-second of February and in the thirteen hundred and fiftieth year from the birth of him who you would have seen or of whose birth you would have heard, had you lived a little longer."[5] Four of the other epistles in this group contain in their dating similar references to the pre-Christian era. The letter to Cicero is "written in the thirteen hundred and forty-fifth year of that God whom you never knew"; that to Seneca "in the thirteen hundred and fiftieth year from the birth of him whom your master preferred to persecute rather than profess."[6]

These expressions show not only that Petrarch was acutely conscious of the distance which separated him from his admired classical authors but also that he realized psychologically at least something of what it meant to live before the Christian era. It does not matter that he was wrong in many of the details of his historical and architectural reconstructions—we now know for example that he was not looking at the actual tomb of Livy at Padua[7]—but it is significant that these phrases in which he dates his letters and places his own position in time reveal the working of a historical imagination. Petrarch knew that Livy knew nothing of Christianity although he would have heard of it had he lived a little longer; he knew also that Quintilian had been employed by the emperor Domitian who persecuted the Christians. But with this knowledge he was able to imagine what these facts meant; he was able to some extent to place the lives and works of these authors in the context of their times; it is not too much to say that he had some conception of anachronism and that this conception underlay his understanding of the fact that no knowledge of Christianity could be attributed to Livy.

We are today so accustomed to applying the test of anachronism to our historical reconstructions that we take it for granted. Every schoolboy knows that Roman senators did not smoke cigars and that Napoleon's troops did not fight with machine guns. The wide diffusion of knowledge about what belongs in particular historical periods does not of course prevent the frequent occurrence of amusing mistakes. The historical novelist who described a moving scene of farewell between father and son in 1356 when the latter declared his intention of going "to fight in the Hundred Years War" forgot that the war could have been so christened only by a later generation.[8] But on the whole we are more conscious than any previous civilization of the succession of historical epochs and of the differences between them. We know that if we are going to construct Colonial Williamsburg as it really was, the streets must be cobbled and the electric wires put under ground. It might indeed be said that in such extreme cases of stage-set reconstruction we commit anachronisms in reverse by requiring modern stores to encase themselves in Queen Anne or Georgian fronts. The very phrase "to commit an anachronism" is furthermore a reminder of the extent to which we think of the concept in pejorative terms. An anachronism is a bad thing. Anachronisms in films, novels, legal and administrative systems are pointed out to be condemned. Anthony Wedgwood Benn in England appealing to the High Court to be allowed to divest himself of his hereditary peerage argues that the condition which prevents his being in the House of Commons is an anachronism which ought to be corrected.[9] The very success of our historical reconstructions, the triumphs of a sense of history, have led us to apply to the realm of ideas the same arguments that are used in determining the "period" of furniture, clothes, architecture or details of daily life. We would all agree with Sir Isaiah Berlin that Hamlet could not have been written at the court of Jenghis Khan and that anyone who asserts it was is not only mistaken but mad.[10] Yet we often too confidently maintain that a particular idea could not have been entertained (because it would have been an anachronism) in the Renaissance, or the Enlightenment or the Victorian era. However certain we may be of our conclusions about the physical environment in history and about the artifacts which have been created by men, we must in the end recognize that there have always been and always will be human anachronisms and this is in fact one of the conditions which prevents the course of history from being as determined as some philosophers have supposed.

This over-developed modern consciousness is the product of a long evolution which may be said to have begun with Petrarch and those of his followers who shared his attitude towards the past. The conception of history which prevailed in the Middle Ages was one of a course of events extending from the creation in the past to the last judgment in the future. Within this unified Christian drama there was small scope for the realization of or interest in differences which divided one period from another, and consequently no conception of anachronism.[11] In the history of art, Professor Panofsky has pointed out the divorce in the Middle Ages between classical form and classical content. Those who worked from literary sources represented ancient gods and goddesses or Greek and Trojan heroes in medieval costumes whereas the artists who had drawn on visual materials dressed Christian figures in classical drapery.[12] Petrarch's attitude represents a decisive change from this medieval way of looking at the past. His letter to Livy does put Livy back into the Roman past in a way which is entirely different from the illustrator of the fourteenth-century French manuscript of Livy who represented the scenes of Roman history as if they were taking place in the France or Burgundy of his own day. The very idea of what is anachronistic, that is, something which is out of its own proper time, whether it is a detail of costume, an idea, an event, or a linguistic expression, rests on a sense of the differences that separate one historical epoch from another. This sense of difference between the present and various periods of the past was of course not as sharp as it later became; we are still far from the historicism of the nineteenth and twentieth centuries. In the drama and the arts anachronisms were not regarded as offensive until after the conquests of romanticism. Yet incomplete as it was, the Renaissance had some sense of the life and style of the past. The humanist followers of Petrarch used the argument from anachronism among others as a weapon of historical criticism.[13] Conversely, the recovery of a sense of classical "style" made possible the imitation of ancient works of art and literature and we remember that Michelangelo's first sculpture was sold as a Roman marble and Alberti circulated a comedy which he had written as a newly found work of Latin literature.[14]

Petrarch's appreciation of the relationship between his own time and the classical past led him also to an interest in projecting the present into the future. One of his latest compositions is the celebrated letter to posterity. In this epistle he speaks directly to us as he had spoken to Livy and the other classical authors: "Greeting. It is possible that some word of me may have come to you, though even this is doubtful, since an insignificant and obscure name will scarcely penetrate far in either time or space. If, however, you should have heard of me, you may desire to know what manner of man I was. . . ."[15] The charming description of Petrarch's physical qualities which follows and the account of his emotional and intellectual development show his desire to project accurate information on himself as an individual to the remotest generations. It may indeed be said that both the letters to ancient authors and the letter to posterity show the same interest in preserving from the distortions of time some portion of the truth.

Petrarch's preoccupation with the destructiveness of time found its most powerful expression in the *Trionfi*. In these allegories which open with the triumph of Love, Chastity triumphs over Love, Death over Chastity, Fame over Death, Time over Fame and finally Eternity over Time. The famous names of history are poisoned by time; lordships and kingdoms fail; time cuts off all that is mortal.

Vidi ogni nostra gloria, al Sol, di neve . . .

Tanto vince e ritoglie il Tempo avaro;
    Chiamasi Fama, ed e morir secondo;
    Ne piu che contra il primo e alcun riparo.

Cosi il Temp trionfa i nomi e'l mondo.[16]

In spite of the ultimate or, rather, penultimate victory of Time
(since Time is in the end itself conquered by Eternity), it was yet
possible for mortals to rescue from time those records of experience which had been preserved by eloquence. It was even possible
to recover works which had been lost in the darkness of time as
Petrarch had himself found the manuscripts of Cicero's letters to
Atticus. The consciousness of the difference between his own time
and republican Rome—the sense of historical perspective—was
accompanied in Petrarch's thought by a re-evaluation of the
traditional judgments on Roman history. The age about which
Livy wrote in the Third Decade of his history, even the age in
which Cicero had lived, appeared clearly to Petrarch's vision as in
some important respects better than the present, and this in spite
of the fact that it lacked the benefit of Christian revelation. In the
letter to Livy as well as in many of his other works Petrarch
approaches the conception of a culturally "dark" or middle age
lying between his own time and antiquity, a conception which
has been so familiar a feature of the periodization of history from
the Renaissance to the present time.[17]

Even in the arena of political life Petrarch at times thought it
possible to apply conceptions resurrected from this Roman past.
The most dramatic occasion on which he intervened was the ill-
starred revolt of Rienzo in Rome in 1347. Niccola or Cola di
Rienzo was the son of a notary whose imagination had been
powerfully affected by what he knew of Roman history and what
he saw of Roman ruins. He had discovered an inscription of the
lex regia by which it was declared that the populus had given over
to the emperor all its imperium et potestas. His opportunity came
when he was sent on a mission to the papal court at Avignon

where he was able to establish relationships with Petrarch on whom his fervent oratory and appeals to the Roman past made a strong impression. Returning to Rome he was able to put himself at the head of a revolutionary movement directed against the domination of the nobility. In a burst of patriotic fervor he declared himself "Nicholas the severe and clement, Tribune of liberty, peace and justice, liberator of the sacred Roman Republic and illustrious prefect of the mother city." In a series of pompous communications to the cities and rulers of Italy and to the pope he announced the restoration of Roman liberty under his rule and the assumption by Rome of the position to which her cultural and political heritage entitled her.[18]

Petrarch was stirred to generous enthusiasm by Rienzo's program and wrote eloquent epistles to Rienzo and to the Roman people. Carried away by his own rhetoric, in one of these communications, he hails Rienzo as the reincarnation of Romulus, Brutus and Camillus. "Hail! Author of Roman liberty, Roman peace and Roman tranquility! To you the present generation owes the fact that it will be able to die in liberty and posterity the fact that it will be born in liberty."[19] This letter was followed by an Eclogue addressed to Rienzo and voicing Petrarch's hopes in a similar manner. Thus the evils of Petrarch's own time were condemned by the standards exhibited by the ancient Romans. Petrarch's appeal to the Roman past reflected the conviction that history, even pagan history, provided a basis for moral criticism. Insofar as the examples of virtue and vice furnished by the past could be imitated and actively realized in the present, history was philosophy teaching by example.

This conception is apparent not only in Petrarch's interventions in active political life which were rather rare, but also in his own historical compositions. His collection of biographies, *De viris illustribus*, was originally conceived to include epitomes of the lives of great men which Petrarch had found scattered through history books. In the version composed in the last years of his life at the request of the tyrant Francesco da Carrara, Petrarch dropped

the pre-Roman lives in accordance with the preference expressed
by the prince, who proposed to decorate a hall of his palace with
the portraits of the subjects of Petrarch's biographies.[20] His
preference for the Romans again shows his sense of the division
which separated classical and early Christian antiquity from the
dark age that followed after. He had earlier expressed his reluc-
tance to include any contemporary or recent figures in his collection of illustrious lives. In a letter to Agapito Colonna written in
1359 he says in answer to the charge that he did not include in his
biographical collection any contemporary figures, "I did not wish
to guide my pen so far and through such darkness."[21] Even, however, when Petrarch did turn to this "darkness" for historical and
biographical material, his purpose remained didactic. *Rerum
memorandum libri* were composed to illustrate a traditional conception of virtue derived from Cicero.[22] According to this tradition, prudence, one of the four cardinal virtues, was divided into
three parts: the memory of things past, the consciousness of things
present and the foreseeing of things to come. The individuals
selected to illustrate these different aspects of prudence are divided
into Roman, non-Roman and modern although the greater
number by far is Roman and illustrates again Petrarch's belief
in the superiority of Roman history as a source of moral
examples.

In spite of the didactic purpose of Petrarch's formal historical
and biographical work, it must not, however, be forgotten that
there was another aspect of his historical interests which in the end
was of far greater importance for European historiography. This
is his appeal for a return to the sources, *ad fontes,* and his concern
for what an ancient author had really said. In his Treatise *On His
Own Ignorance* he condemns "the stupid Aristotelians, who day by
day in every single word they speak do not cease to hammer into
the heads of others Aristotle whom they know by name only."[23] A
great part of Petrarch's career was dedicated to his attempt to
recover accurate texts of his beloved classical authors. If he was
convinced that the history of Livy provided examples for the

present, he was equally convinced that it was necessary to know precisely what Livy had said so far as this was possible after the destruction wrought by time and barbarians. We have only recently come to know through the researches of Professor Billanovich how much Petrarch contributed to the establishment of the text of Livy.[24] Petrarch early copied one of the most important manuscripts of Livy, now known as the Harleian at Oxford and dedicated himself to the reconstruction of the best possible text. "The tradition of Livy during the Renaissance," says Professor Billanovich, "was for the most part the tradition which Petrarch himself had formed. By means of a fortunate comparison of texts, he corrected the books of the first *Decade*; which, although descended from a single archetype, had been transmitted through divergent channels. And he managed to obtained the fourth *Decade* when it had only just reached Avignon."[25] Throughout his life Livy remained for Petrarch his favorite historian.

It may be pointed out that this effort to establish with the aid of grammar and philology what Livy or another ancient author had really written stopped a good deal short of what we understand by historical research. For Petrarch Livy *was* Roman history and there was no question of going behind his narrative to investigate what had actually happened through a process of comparing different documents and different kinds of evidence.[26] Nevertheless the attempt to recover a correct text did involve coming into more direct contact with the character, personality, style and idiosyncrasies of the author—Livy was felt as a more real historical personage than had been the case in the middle ages.[27] Furthermore, the comparison of two or more manuscripts was at least the beginning of criticism even if the scope was limited to the recovery of one narrative history rather than the reconstruction of a past through the testimony of many.[28]

There may thus be distinguished in Petrarch's attitude towards history three different components. There is first the sense of historical distance, the consciousness of the differences between classical antiquity and the Christian era which followed with the dawning realization that this great gap in time and circumstances could be bridged by an effort of the imagination. Secondly, there is the conception that to the extent to which this past can be recovered, it provides moral lessons for a future generation. History is philosophy teaching by example in which the past, if correctly understood, informs and instructs the present. Thirdly, there is the basis for that correct understanding, that is, history as the intellectual conquest of what an ancient author had really said derived from a critical and philological study of the texts. Our modern habits of thought about history tend in general to make a sharp separation between these latter two components. Much that may be discovered by research is irrelevant to any "lessons" of history and conversely many moral and political "truths" cannot be supported by historical evidence or at any rate by historical evidence alone. In the minds of Petrarch and his immediate followers, however, there cannot be said to have been any sense of incompatibility between these two components of the historian's activity. For most of the characteristic thinkers of the Renaissance the cry for the return to the sources was accompanied by the conviction that the sources when recovered would be relevant to present concerns. Criticism and a program for moral and educational reform sustained each other, and until they began to be separated provided the basis of the hopes of the humanist publicists.

The intellectual impulse given by Petrarch to historical studies can be traced in succeeding generations. Editions and translations of ancient historians were produced in increasing numbers and many humanists wrote histories modelled on Livy. The study of history was elevated to an important and sometimes to a central place in the educational curriculum. The Florentine chancellor, Coluccio Salutati, one of Petrarch's great admirers, wrote in 1392, a letter to the Grand Master of the Order of St. John of Jerusalem praising him for his valuable collection of books. Among these he singled out for particular mention the histories and commended the Grand Master for having "cherished the historians whose duty it is to hand down to posterity the memory of things done so that the examples of kings, nations, and illustrious men can be either equalled or exceeded by imitating them. . . . The knowledge of things done warns princes, teaches people, and instructs individuals. . . . It is the most certain basis for the conduct of affairs. History teaches us the doctrines of philosophy. What is rhetoric itself, one of the most beautiful of the sciences, but the conflict and opposition between things which have been done and things which ought to have been done?"[29] Salutati's emphasis on rhetoric is significant. The claims of rhetoric against the position of medieval dialectic were one of the means by which the humanists strove to advance their cause. Only through the genius of eloquence exercised in the arrangement and disposition of the material could historians save events and individuals from the ravages of time and make fully effective the lessons to be learned.[30]

The judgment of Salutati was confirmed by the formal treatises on education. Pier Paolo Vergerio, for example, whose *De ingenuis moribus* is of the beginning of the fifteenth century, declares in his discussion of the ideal curriculum: "We come now to the consideration of the various subjects which ought to be included under the name of liberal studies. Among these I accord the first place to history on the grounds both of its attractiveness and its utility, qualities which appeal equally to the scholar and the statesman. . . . History, then, gives us the concrete examples of the principles inculcated by philosophy. The one shows what men should do, the other what men have said and done in the past and what practical lessons men may draw therefrom for the present day."[31] Such a text as this clearly reveals the consequences of Petrarch's approach to historical studies: there was no gulf between the study and the market place, no divorce between culture and politics.

The most celebrated Italian historian of the first part of the fifteenth century affirmed the same ideas in both his life and his work. As Florentine chancellor and successor to Salutati, Leonardo Bruni endeavored to put into practice the lessons on civic liberty which he, as a scholar, had learned from Roman history.[32] He believed that he ought to leave behind him a history of his own epoch so that future generations could draw from it the same kind of lessons as he had drawn from the study of the classical world. "I feel that I have an obligation," he wrote at the beginning of his *Rerum suorum tempore gestarum*, "to this age of mine, to give some notice of it to posterity in whatsoever light it may appear in the future. If only those who lived before us and who had some literary ability had done this, we would not today find ourselves in such a state of darkness and ignorance. Indeed it appears to me that the ages of Cicero and Demosthenes are much better known than that of sixty years ago."[33] Thus Bruni combined an effort to extend his knowledge of the past with the exaltation of the lessons which had been learned from Roman history. In developing further the periodization which had been suggested by Petrarch he bore witness to the sense of emergence from a time of darkness which was so characteristic of many of his contemporaries.[34]

These views on history and particularly on Roman history as a source of moral example were adopted by educators. Most influential among those who founded new schools or reformed the traditional curricula was Vittorino da Feltre, the beloved schoolmaster of Mantua. Vittorino had been educated in the full tide of enthusiasm for grammar, rhetoric, history, poetry, and moral philosophy as against logic, dialectic and natural philosophy. He revolted against the moral and intellectual tone of the University of Padua where he taught for a time and subsequently opened his own school in Venice. Thence he was summoned to Mantua by the Marquis Gonzaga who entrusted to Vittorino the education of his children. The *Casa Giocosa* established in a Gonzaga villa became the model for educational reform and for the fullest development of the program of the early humanists. Among its pupils were to be found the children of poor families as well as the princes of the house of Gonzaga. Vittorino was also an innovator in providing equal opportunities for girls as for boys. The ideals of his program reflected a fusion of classic and Christian traditions and he inculcated above all the precepts of service to the state and society whether in the active life of a statesman or in the contemplative life of religious vocation. He won the affectionate devotion of all his pupils and perhaps the monument which best characterizes his achievement is the medal of Pisanello with the sensitive portrait and the inscription, "Summus mathematicus et omnis humanitatis pater," while on the obverse is the representation of a pelican opening its breast to feed its young, a traditional symbol of sacrifice.[35]

In this school a great importance was accorded to the study of history and Livy remained always for Vittorino as he had been for Petrarch one of the most cherished authors. The pupils learned to read aloud and memorize passages from Livy and discussed the heroes of Roman history in the spirit in which Petrarch had collected his exemplary biographies. The results of this education can be followed in the later lives of two of his pupils, Giovanni Andrea Bussi, Bishop of Aleria and Federigo da Montefeltro, Duke of Urbino.

The Bishop of Aleria in Corsica served four popes as acolyte, secretary and librarian, and although he was rewarded with two Corsican bishoprics, Alessio and Aleria, he never visited his sees. He enjoys the remarkable distinction of having collaborated with the first Roman printers Sweynheim and Pannartz at Subiaco and at Rome in the publishing of the *editiones principes* of a large number of Latin authors including Livy.[36] In the preface to the Livy of 1469 he traces his first acquaintance with Livy to Vittorino's school and professes that he owes most of his knowledge of the text to Vittorino who had been the first to introduce him to Petrarch's work on Livy. He pays touching tribute to Vittorino as the "Socrates of our age," and as *"sapientiae magister, honestatis specimen, bonitatis examplus, divitiarum contemptor."*[37] This famous edition appearing within five years of the centenary of the death of Petrarch is an eloquent testimony to the fruit of Petrarch's interest in the text of Livy. By an invention of which Petrarch could not even have dreamed his textual reconstruction which had descended to Vittorino and to Valla was now reproduced in a manner which would make it available to all readers and scholars.

The most famous pupil of Vittorino was Federigo da Monte-feltro, Count and subsequently Duke of Urbino. Federigo whose profile with the nicked nose is familiar to us from the many contemporary portraits offers the ideal example of the Renaissance prince. He distinguished himself at an early age as a military strategist and commander of men and served at various times in the employ of Venice, Florence and the papacy as well as fighting his own battles. As a ruler he organized in his territories an efficient administration and provided justice for his subjects. As a patron of arts and letters he built the great ducal palace at Urbino, a most perfect example of fifteenth-century domestic architecture, and employed for its decoration the most gifted artists he could find. To fill his library he commissioned the Florentine bookseller Vespasiano da Bisticci to hire an army of copyists to make the most beautiful manuscripts of the Greek, Roman and Christian classics which he wished to possess.[38] Although as a youth he had studied for only two years at Vittorino's school, he never forgot his master and in the study at the ducal palace where were enshrined portraits of the worthies of all ages there was included Berruguete's portrait of Vittorino with an inscription recording the gratitude of the duke. It was undoubtedly in Vittorino's school that he acquired the interest in reading Roman history which he always retained. Vespasiano, who greatly admired Federigo, included a brief life of him in his collections of lives of illustrious men. In this life he tells us that the Duke of Urbino observed a daily routine of public reading of Livy at mealtime. "When the duke had sat down the doors would be left open, so that all might enter, and he never ate except the hall were full, some one would always read to him; during Lent a spiritual work, and at other times the *Histories* of Livy, all in Latin."[39] Thus we may see that the same teaching deriving ultimately from Petrarch had served as a stimulus for Andrea Bussi who edited the text of Livy and for Federigo da Montefeltro who reflected on the lessons to be derived from studying him. What the scholar elucidated the statesman applied. Nothing could testify more strongly to the strength of the conviction of the importance of historical studies and the relevance of the lessons of history.

When we reach the sixteenth century there is a break and it is signalized by Machiavelli. We know that Machiavelli was exposed during his early years to the traditional admiration for Livy. His father Bernardo tells in his *Libri di Ricordi* of the contract with the Florentine book binder for the binding of his copy of Livy and of the payment made by his "figliuolo Niccolo."[40] In this copy Niccolo probably began his intensive reading in Livy, no doubt suspended during the time when he was employed as secretary of the Florentine chancery, but again resumed during his period of enforced leisure and culminating in the writing of the *Discourses* in 1516–1517.[41] We are astonished, however, to find that Machiavelli writes at the beginning of the *Discourses* a condemnation of the way in which history had been taught. He considers that his predecessors have failed and begins by announcing the originality of his own approach. "I have decided," says Machiavelli, "to enter on a path which up to now has been trodden by no one, and if it brings me labor and difficulty it may bring me reward. . . ." He is astonished and grieved that examples from the history of antiquity are more admired than imitated. And the more so because in the study of the civil law or in medicine, "recourse is always had to those judgments or to those remedies which have been decreed or provided by the ancients, since the civil law is nothing else than the opinion of ancient jurisconsults, which opinions, when they are arranged in order, teach our present jurisconsults to judge." If the jurisconsults can be taught to judge according to a body of laws derived from the history of their profession, why cannot rulers be taught to rule? Machiavelli declares that he is convinced that this failure to profit by the example of the ancient world in the business of ruling men is due "not so much to the weakness to which the present religion has conducted the world nor to the evils that a proud indolence has brought on many Christian cities and provinces as to a lack of a true knowledge of history, through not extracting the sense of it when reading it and not savoring the knowledge that it has in itself."[42]

Considering the number of appeals to the value of studying history which had been uttered by the humanist educators from the time of Petrarch to that of Machiavelli himself, this indictment appears the more curious. Surely Machiavelli knew that these educators had recommended the study of antiquity for its exemplary character and had pored over it in an effort "to extract the sense of it." The key to Machiavelli's condemnation, however, is to be found not in what the humanists professed but in what they had failed to accomplish. Looking at the political disorder which had come upon Florence and indeed upon all Italy since the French invasion of 1494, Machiavelli was above all impressed with the contrast between what was preached and what was practiced. He did not condemn a teacher like Vittorino or a ruler like Federigo because he had tried to make the study of history applicable to the present but because they had not succeeded. The easy confidence of an earlier generation that it was enough to find out what the lessons of history were and that they would be relevant to the present was beginning to crack. It is in this connection most significantly that Machiavelli appeals to the disciplines of jurisprudence and medicine as those which represent the successful use of antiquity.

Machiavelli, whose father was a lawyer, was impressed with the fact that in both medicine and the law the particular case was assimilated to a general rule, and this general rule had been tested by many authorities of classical antiquity. Those who had contemplated the course of history had indeed found examples of virtue and vice, wisdom and foolishness but these had never been reduced to a system; there existed no systematic body of knowledge which could be compared to that accumulated by the commentators on the civil law and this was the focal point of Machiavelli's criticism of the humanist tradition—a tradition from which he had himself started and upon which he had built but which he found wanting as he reflected on the failures of Italian political institutions to meet the shock of the northern invasions.

Machiavelli's appeal to the lawyers was founded on a recognition of their prestige and practical success. It is a little like the argument one often hears today that the teachers of law and medicine know what they want and can impart it so that they produce a body of effectively trained students whereas the teachers of the humanities are vague and inconclusive with the result that their students tend to be a group of ineffectual dilettantes. In the Italian universities of the late Middle Ages and Renaissance the courses on the civil and canon law drew more students than did those on any other subject.

In citing the success of the profession of jurisprudence Machiavelli thus recognized a fact of the current social scene and the same was true to perhaps a lesser degree of the profession of medicine. Nevertheless his appeal to the lawyers contains an element of paradox. Machiavelli was pleading for both "history" and "system" but the very jurisconsults who most completely realized the ideal of a systematic body of knowledge, applicable to the present, were the least historical.

The greatest figure in the late medieval school of Italian jurisprudence had been Bartolus of Sassoferrato (1314–1357) whose authority was so great that his opinions were cited by rulers and by courts as if they had the authority of judicial decisions.[43] Bartolus and his followers—the so-called Post-Glossators—were much more interested in the elaboration and application of a system of rules than they were in the achievement of any historical understanding of the growth of law or even of the existence of different periods in the history of institutions. For them the *Corpus* of Justinian was still *de jure* applicable to a Roman empire that had not ceased to exist. It was only necessary to take account of the *de facto* variations which made necessary subtle and elaborate adjustments in the universal rules to fit them to particular contemporary conditions. They did not feel that sense of distance either from the age of Justinian or from the classical jurists behind Justinian which we have seen dawning in the thought of Petrarch. In a word their thought may be said to have remained fundamen-

tally medieval in its conception of the relationship between antiquity and the contemporary scene.

This school still dominated the teaching of law in the Italian
universities in the sixteenth century.[44] Ever since the time of
Petrarch, however, its methods and conclusions had been under
attack by the humanists. Petrarch's views were forcibly expressed
in a letter he wrote in 1340 to a young man from Genoa who had
requested advice about going into the law as a career. Although
Petrarch had himself begun by studying the civil law like many
others who afterwards became men of letters, he had revolted
against it and he now replied to his young friend with arguments
against the lawyers. Petrarch related that he had spent seven years
in the study of the law, first at Montpellier and subsequently at
Bologna. "If you ask," he wrote, "whether I regret this time
today, I say that I do. For I wish to have seen all things so far as
it may be permitted to me and I regret and will regret, as long as
there is breath in me so large a part of my life passed by. For I
could have done anything else during these years which would
have been more noble or more suited to my nature." Recognizing
that great glory was formerly sought and achieved by individuals
in the study of the civil law, he cites examples from antiquity such
as Solon, who, however, as he does not fail to point out, in his old
age gave himself to the study of poetry. "The greater part of our
legists," he declares, "who care nothing for knowing about the
origins of law and about the founders of jurisprudence, and have
no other preoccupation than to gain as much as they can from
their profession, are content to learn whatever is written in
the law about contracts, judgments or wills, and it never
occurs to them that the knowledge of arts and of origins and of
literature would be of the greatest practical use for their very
profession."[45]

The accusations that the lawyers were unhistorical and that they
had no interest in the arts were repeated many times by Petrarch's
followers. Boccaccio, Salutati, Bruni, Poggio Bracciolini, Maffeo
Vegio and many others joined in what became a veritable

polemic against the lawyers.[46] Among these attacks the most in-
cisive was that delivered against Bartolus by Lorenzo Valla in
1433. In that year the young humanist scholar, already a prodigy
who dazzled his contemporaries, had been invited to a chair of
rhetoric at the University of Pavia. Like the other Italian universities of this period Pavia contained a faculty of arts and a faculty of
law, the latter of which included both civil and canon law. Each
faculty had its own organization and its own rector and there had
developed considerable rivalry between the two schools. Valla
one day encountered a group of law professors who were lavishing
uncritical praise on the Bartolists. Someone in the company made
the provocative remark that one small treatise of Bartolus, the
De insigniis et armis was better than all the works of Cicero put
together. Valla made an incredulous reply and then immediately
sought out a friend from whom he borrowed a copy of the
treatise of Bartolus which he read with a growing sense of indignation and amazement that anyone could have made such a
comparison. He then sat down and directed a letter to his friend
Sacco who, although on the law faculty, shared Valla's ideas on
the value of humanist learning and on correct Latin. In this letter
Valla expressed his condemnation of Bartolus' treatise in the
strongest language. He began by bewailing the times in which
anyone could have preferred a barbarous work of jurisprudence to
the golden tongue of Cicero. He pointed out that even in the title
of the Bartolist treatise there was an egregious error: "*insigniis*"
should have been "*insignibus.*" He described Bartolus as an "ass,"
"idiot," and "madman," and found his work completely lacking
in an understanding of Roman law and institutions. The emperor
Justinian, whose work had occasioned so many commentaries, was
really to blame and our attention ought rather to be directed to
the true sources, to the jurists of the classical period. Valla had
originally directed his letter to his friend, Sacco, but in order to
get a wider circulation for his views, he subsequently redirected
it to the Milanese humanist, Piero Candido Decembrio. The
letter immediately created such hostility among the conservative

faction in Pavia that Valla was forced to resign his chair and flee the city.[47]

The humanists continued their attacks on the traditional teaching of the law throughout the fifteenth century and, impatient with the failure of the lawyers to reform, they began themselves to apply to the legal sources techniques of philological and historical criticism. Before the end of the century the great Angelo Poliziano had proposed a critical edition of the famous Florentine manuscript of the *Pandects*.[48] And by the time when Machiavelli was beginning his *Discorsi*, Andrea Alciatus was already demonstrating that historical and literary evidence could be applied to the understanding of legal texts. The first publication of Alciatus was his *Annotationes in tres posteriores Codicis Iustiniani libros* in 1515 which with the *Annotationes in Pandectas* of Budé published in France seven years earlier marked the coming of age of the school of humanistic jurisprudence.[49] Although Alciatus himself was never dogmatic or extreme in condemning the Bartolist school and was willing to recognize the valid achievements of his predecessors, some of his followers adopted *in toto* the humanist criticisms and proclaimed that a knowledge of grammar and philology provided the only sound approach to the study of the law.

Thus by the second decade of the sixteenth century there were already coming to be distinguished two schools of interpretation in legal studies. The first or traditional school afterwards known as the *mos italicus* emphasized the application to the present of rules derived from the analysis of the authoritative texts of antiquity. The second which came to be known as the *mos gallicus* (because widely adopted by the French legal scholars) devoted itself to the historical understanding of the classical law with all the resources that history and philology could supply, but without regard to the application of the results to the present.[50] The aim of the former was systematic, that of the latter historical. When Machiavelli held up the example of jurisprudence to those humanists whom he accused of having failed in their teaching of history, he was in a sense taking a step backward. The *Discorsi* are in respect to their attitude towards history nearer Bartolus than they are to Machiavelli's contemporary, Alciatus. Although Machiavelli shared with the fifteenth century humanist tradition the interest in Roman history and the concentration on Livy, he did not believe that examples derived from understanding the text of Livy would produce lessons applicable to the present unless they were systematized. Although he started from the humanist interest in history as it had been initiated by Petrarch, he repudiated the confident humanist assumption that increased admiration and understanding of the text of Livy would automatically be followed by lessons which could be applied to the improvement of the individual and of society in this own time. This assumption which as we have seen had been held in the fifteenth century by such educators as Vittorino and such rulers as Federigo was perhaps first weakened by the growth, initiated by the humanist scholars themselves, of two schools of interpreting the legal tradition. It was, however, further undermined by Machiavelli's great appeal for the necessity for systematization from historical materials. What had begun in the early Renaissance as a conception of history that combined a real interest in the past with a belief in its relevance to the present was now in the process of being separated into what was to become the "merely historical" on the one hand and the materials of theoretical structures, political, social or constitutional, on the other. In the period after Machiavelli the consequences of that separation became clearer in the north than in Italy and it is perhaps most dramatically illustrated in France.

Jean Bodin published in 1566 the most philosophical book on the nature of historical thought written in the sixteenth century. At the beginning of this work he distinguished three kinds of history, divine, natural and human, which corresponded to three kinds of knowledge, faith, science and prudence. In the realm of human history, "which flows from the will of men which is ever variable,"[51] prudence may be acquired by a comparative study of civilizations with a view to eliciting the general rules of social behaviours which may be applied to recurring situations. Like Machiavelli before him, he wished to understand the true meaning of ancient history by finding in it examples which had a universal validity. Both of them might be described today as retrospective sociologists. The longest chapter in Bodin's book is devoted to the consideration of the foundations of states and of changes in their constitutions which Bodin considers to be the principal subject matter of history. In this endeavor he finds himself hindered by those who prefer to call themselves grammarians rather than juriconsults. "We must not look for salvation," he says in a very interesting passage, "to those whom no one deigns to consult in matters of law, to those who prefer to consider themselves grammarians rather than juriconsults, or to those . . . who expect from the power of words alone the safety of the establishment of justice, and the resolution of conflicts. This plague of grammar has in our day so inserted itself into all our disciplines that we have to endure under the guise of philosophers, orators, mathematicians and even theologians, petty grammarians who are barely out of school. Those who ought to have confined themselves to cleaning the dirt and spots from ancient pictures so as to make the original painting appear, have taken a steel dagger and made such huge and indelible marks on all the books that the image of antiquity can hardly any longer be seen."[52] How we seem to hear the voice of Machiavelli in the indictment of those "who expect from the power of words alone the safety of the state!" But Bodin's repudiation of a part of the humanist tradition goes farther. To condemn the study of grammar for having obscured the image of antiquity was to condemn what had been for the humanists the most important instrument for historical reconstruction. The substance of the complaints against Bartolus of such critics as Petrarch and Valla had been that he did not know language and that this made it impossible for him to understand history. Now Bodin feels that it is the linguistic purists who have destroyed the vision of the past.

Bodin's argument was directed not only against his humanist

predecessors but also against his contemporaries. Among them was one whose pre-eminence as a scholar of the law was unquestioned. Jacques Cujas particularly dedicated his scholarship to the restoration of juridical texts of the pre-Justinian period, and in this he followed faithfully the direction in which Valla's work had pointed. His critical editions and learned commentaries include the discovery and study of interpolations in the text of Justinian's *Corpus* and his principal weapon was precisely that knowledge of grammar, that philology which Bodin had condemned. In the case of Cujas, however, the clearer the image of antiquity became, the less applicable to the modern world did it seem to be, and this was the point of Bodin's criticism. The story is told of Cujas that when his pupils came to him to ask what course they should follow in the terrible crises of the religious struggle, he replied, *"Nihil hoc ad edictum praetoris."* This had nothing to do with the edict of the praetor.[53] By these words Cujas meant in the first place that religious problems ought not to be subject to civil legislation but secondly and more profoundly that it was his task to teach history and not to draw from it lessons for the present or the future. The image of antiquity had been recovered but at the same time it ceased to speak directly to the modern world. History was becoming academic. What it discovered might be archeologically true but it was irrelevant to the concerns of a later age. The opposition between Bodin and Cujas would have been incomprehensible to a Petrarch or a Valla. These humanists would not have understood Bodin's condemnation of grammar as a tool of historical understanding or Cujas' lack of interest in the application of the results of historical understanding. For about two hundred years—roughly the period between Petrarch and Erasmus—the humanist tradition just as it believed in the compatibility of classic and Christian was able to also combine a deeper historical knowledge of the classical past with an undiminished confidence in the relevance of the lessons of the past. But by the time Cujas gave his response to his students, this phase of the Renaissance was over.

NOTES

1. Carl Becker, "Everyman His Own Historian," *The American Historical Review*, XXXVII (1931–32), pp. 221–236. See especially p. 226.

2. For a survey of attitudes towards primitive society see A. O. Lovejoy, *Related Ideas in Antiquity* (Baltimore, 1935).

3. Perhaps the best introduction to the present state of the question and the bibliography is the essay by F. Chabod, "The Concept of the Renaissance," in *Machiavelli and the Renaissance* (Harvard University Press, 1958), pp. 149–247.

4. An effective statement of this view is contained in H. Trevor-Roper, "The General Crisis of the Seventeenth Century," *Past and Present*, No. 16 (Nov. 1959), pp. 31–64.

5. Petrarch, *Epistolae de rebus familiaribus et variae*, 3 vols. J. Fracassetti, ed. (Florence, 1859–63), III, p. 282. My translation.

6. *Ibid.*, 263, 280.

7. B. Ullman, "The Post-Mortem Adventures of Livy," *Studies in the Italian Renaissance* (Rome, 1955), pp. 55–79.

8. I owe this reference to Professor B. J. Whiting.

9. *The New York Times*, July 29, 1961.

10. I. Berlin, "History and Theory: The Concept of Scientific History," *History and Theory: Studies in the Philosophy of History*, I: 5 (1960).

11. Eva M. Sanford, "The Study of Ancient History in the Middle Ages," *Journal of the History of Ideas*, V (1944), pp. 21–43.

12. Erwin Panofsky, *Renaissance and Renascences in Western Art* (Stockholm, 1961). See especially chapter II, pp. 42–133; also the author's earlier article, "Renaissance and Renascences," in *The Kenyon Review*, VI (1944), p. 201–306.

13. For example, Lorenzo Valla in his *De falso credita et ementita Constantini donatione*, W. Schwahn, ed. (Berlin, 1927). See p. 44, "*Iste non putat illud nisi ex auro esse, cui circulus aureus nunc cum gemmis apponi a regibus solet.*" There is a discussion of Valla as a historian in F. Gaeta, *Lorenzo Valla: Filologia e storia nell' umanesimo Italiano* (Naples, 1955), pp. 129–192. Gaeta's view of Valla's significance is criticized by Hanna H. Gray, "History and Rhetoric in Quattrocento Humanism" (unpub. diss., Radcliffe College, 1957), especially in chap. IV.

14. On Michelangelo, see Charles De Tolnay, *The Youth of Michelangelo* (Princeton, 1947), p. 27 and note 88. On Alberti, G. Mancini, *Vita di Leon Battista Alberti* (Florence, 1911), pp. 54–55.

15. The latest and best edition of this letter is in Petrarch, *Prose*, ed. by G. Martellotti (Milan, 1955), pp. 2–19. The quotation is from the English translation by James H. Robinson in *Petrarch, the First Modern Man* (New York, 1909), p. 59.

16. Petrarch, *I Trionfi* (Florence, 1908), pp. 105–106.

17. See T. Mommsen, "Petrarch's Conception of the Dark Ages," *Speculum* XVII (1943), pp. 226–249.

18. On Rienzo see Paul Piur, *Cola di Rienzo* (Milan, 1934) and Iris Origo, *Tribune of Rome; A Biography of Cola di Rienzo* (London, 1938). Rienzo's correspondence has been edited with an extensive commentary by Konrad Burdach in *Vom Mittelalter zur Reformation: Forschungen zur Geschichte der Deutschen Bildung*, Vol. II, Part III, *Briefwechsel des Cola di Rienzo* (Berlin, 1912).

19. Burdach, *Briefwechsel des Cola di Rienzo*, p. 95. The Eclogue to Rienzo, pp. 87–93.

20. E. H. Wilkin's, *Petrarch's Later Years* (Cambridge, Mass., March, 1959), pp. 283–302.

21. *Le Familiari*, XX, 8. Quoted by T. Mommsen, "Petrarch's Conception of the Dark Ages," *Speculum*, XVII (1943), pp. 226–249.

22. *Rerum memorandum libri*, G. Billanovich, ed. (Florence, 1945), Introduction, pp. cixxiv-cxxx.

23. Petrarch, "On His Own Ignorance," Hans Nachod, tr., in *The Renaissance Philosophy of Man*, Paul O. Kristeller and John H. Randall, Jr., eds. (Chicago, 1945), p. 107.

24. G. Billanovich, "Petrarch and the Textual Tradition of Livy," *Journal of the Warburg Institute*, XIV (1951), pp. 125 ff.

25. *Ibid.*, p. 172.

26. Cf. Hanna H. Gray, unpub. diss., especially chap. IV.

27. On the "taking contact" with the personalities of the past see E. Garin *"La storia nel pensiero del rinascimento,"* in *Medioevo e Rinascimento* (Bari, 1954), pp. 194-210, especially p. 204.

28. On the use of critical methods by humanist historians see B. Ullman, "Leonardo Bruni and Humanist Historiography," *Studies in the Renaissance* (Rome, 1955), pp. 321-344.

29. Salutati, *Epistolario di Coluccio Salutati*, Novati, ed. (Rome, 1891-1905), II, pp. 289-295. My translation.

30. See Hanna H. Gray's discussion of the relation between history and rhetoric.

31. P. P. Vergerio, *De ingenuis Morbius et liberalibus studiis adolescentiae*, A. Onesotto, ed. (Padua, 1918), p. 121. English translation by W. H. Woodward, *Vittorino da Feltre and other Renaissance Educators* (Cambridge, England, 1918), p. 106.

32. See, for the most thorough discussion of the ideas of Bruni and his circle, the two volume work by Hans Baron, *The Crisis of the Early Italian Renaissance: Civic Humanism and Republican Liberty in an Age of Classicism and Tyranny* (Princeton, 1955), especially Volume I, pp. 163-240.

33. Leonardo Bruni, *Rerum suo tempore gestarum commentarius*, E. Santini and C. di Pierro, eds., *Rerum Italicarum Scriptores*, XIX, Part 3 (Citta di Castillo, p. 432.

34. See B. L. Ullman, "Leonardo Bruni and Humanist Historiography," in *Studies in the Italian Renaissance* (Rome, 1955), pp. 321-344.

35. On Vittorino and his school see W. H. Woodward, *Vittorino da Feltre*, and E. Garin, *L'educazione in Europa* (1400-1600), (Bari, 1957), pp. 147-153.

36. On Andrea Bussi, see *Enciclopedia Italiana* (Milan, 1929—) art. "Bussi" and H. Quentin, *Essais de critique textuelle* (Paris, 1926), p. 27 ff.

37. Livy, *Historiae Romanae Decades*, J. Andreas, ed. (Rome, 1469), Preface.

38. On Federigo, see James Dennistown, *Memoirs of the Dukes of Urbino*, 3 vols. (London, 1909). This is a new edition with notes by Edward Hutton.

39. Vespasiano da Bisticci, *Vita di nomini illustri*, L. Frati, ed. (Bologna, 1892), p. 308. English translation by W. G. and E. Waters (London, 1926), p. 108; Harper Torchbook edition, 1963.

40. Bernardo Machiavelli, *Libro di Ricordi*, C. Olschki, ed. (Florence, 1954), p. 222.

41. For the date of the *Discourses* see Hans Baron, "Machiavelli the Republican Citizen and the Author of 'The Prince'," *English Historical Review* lxxvi (1961), pp. 217-253.

42. Quotations from Machiavelli, *The Prince and the Discourses*, with an Introduction by Max Lerner (Modern Library, New York, 1940), pp. 104-105.

43. On Bartolus, see C. S. N. Woolf, *Bartolus of Sassoferrato* (Cambridge, 1913).

44. On the law faculties in the Italian universities see B. Brugi, *Per la storia della giurisprudenza e delle università italiane: Saggi* (Turin, 1915), and *Nuovi Saggi* (Turin, 1921).

45. Petrarch, *Epistolae de rebus familiaribus et variae*, J. Frascasetti, ed. 3 vols. (Florence, 1859-63), III, pp. 14-15. My translation.

46. For an account of this literature see Maffei, *Gli inizi del'umanesimo giuridico*, esp. pp. 33-81.

47. L. Valla, *Contra Bartolum libellum cui titulus de insigniis et armis epistola* (Basel, 1518). On this work see Gaeta, *Lorenzo Valla* (Naples, 1955), pp. 195–197, and Maffei, *Gli inizi del'umanesimo giuridico*, pp. 38–41.

48. F. Buonamici, *Il Poliziano giureconsulto* (Pisa, 1863).

49. On Alciato, see P. E. Viard, *André Alciat 1492–1550* (Paris, 1926) and on Budé, Louis Delaruelle, *Guillaume Budé, les origines, les débuts, les idées maitresses* (Paris, 1907).

50. On *mos italicus* and *mos gallicus* see G. Astuti, *Mos italicus et mos gallicus nei dialogui "de iuris interpretibus" di Alberico Gentili* (Bologna, 1937) and G. Kisch, *Humanismus und Jurisprudenz, Der Kampf zwischen mos italicus und mos gallicus an der Universität Basel* (Basel, 1955). See also G. Kisch, *Erasmus und die Jurisprudenz seiner Zeit* (Basel, 1906).

51. Jean Bodin, *Methodus ad facilem historiarum in Oeuvres Philosophiques de Jean Bodin*, P. Mesnard, ed. (Paris, 1951), p. 115. My translation.

52. *Ibid.*, p. 109.

53. Letter of Alexander Scot, *"Ad lectorem,"* prefaced to Jacques Cujas *Opera omnia* (Lyon, 1606), fo 3r.

PAUL OSKAR KRISTELLER ～ *Renaissance*
Platonism

HEN WE THINK OF THAT PERIOD IN WESTERN
history which we are accustomed to call the
Renaissance and which extends approximate-
ly from 1300 to 1600, we are not likely to
remember its philosophical thought, but
rather its achievements in the arts and in
the sciences, or the political, social, and religious developments
which occurred during those three centuries. To be sure, it seems
appropriate to ask whether a period so distinguished in other
fields of civilization also left an impact on the history of philosophy, or what philosophical ideas, if any, formed a part of the
general background of the art and literature, the political and
religious thought of the Renaissance. During the last hundred
years or so, more and more specialists have begun to explore
these questions, and their results would seem to deserve some
attention. Yet, while many more problems in this area remain
still unexplored, even what has been ascertained is largely ignored, not only by the general public, but also by many students
of philosophy and history alike. Ever since Jacob Burckhardt,[1]
most general historians of the Renaissance have paid scanty attention to the philosophical thought of the period, whereas historians
of philosophy in their courses and textbooks still tend to jump

[103]

with a few perfunctory and often misleading remarks from Thomas Aquinas or William of Ockham to Bacon and Descartes. There are some plausible reasons for this state of affairs. The Renaissance does not seem to have produced any philosophers of the very first order, and although there were many interesting thinkers, their work seems to lack permanent significance because it was superseded when modern science and modern philosophy received a new and more solid foundation in the seventeenth century through Galileo and Kepler, Bacon and Descartes. Moreover, in the Renaissance, more than in some other periods, the progress of thought seems to have been due not only to the professional and professed philosophers, but also to many poets and artists, scholars and scientists who thought and wrote about philosophical problems without being philosophers in the technical sense of the term. Finally, and this is another aspect of the same problem, the content and task of philosophy, and its relations to such other disciplines as theology and literature, mathematics and medicine, were conceived in a manner that is markedly different from other periods of philosophy, and especially from our own contemporary type of philosophy.[2] It will be well to keep in mind these difficulties when we try to understand one of the major philosophical movements of the Renaissance period: Platonism.

Unlike the term "humanism" which requires a good deal of clarification, the term "Platonism" seems to be self-explanatory: it indicates a current or school of philosophy inspired by the writings and teachings of Plato. Yet Plato's philosophy is quite complex and sometimes obscure, and his doctrine as it is expressed in his dialogues shows a number of gaps and inconsistencies. No wonder that it was subjected already in antiquity to a variety of selections and interpretations, as well as to amalgamations with alien ideas of diverse origin. Consequently, the history of Platonism has not been a constant repetition of ideas first formulated by Plato, but rather a series of very different variations on a common theme. Thus it is by no means easy to bring all forms of Platonism, even within a limited period such as the Renaissance, under a simple formula. Different thinkers may be called Platonists for very different reasons, and it is incumbent upon the historian to penetrate beyond the label and to determine in each instance which ideas, Platonic or non-Platonic in origin, characterize the thought of a given philosopher.[3]

According to the view held by most older historians, the period of the Renaissance was characterized by a revival of Platonism as against the dominant Aristotelianism of the Middle Ages. More recently we have learned that Platonism was very much alive during the Middle Ages, and that Aristotelianism continued to be very strong during the Renaissance. Thus the novelty and significance of Renaissance Platonism have become problematic, and we must try to understand it more adequately in the light of the new information that has been made available by recent scholarly investigation.

If we want to find the sources and antecedents of Renaissance Platonism, we must look in more than one direction. One of them is no doubt that medieval Platonism or Augustinianism which culminated in the Latin West during the twelfth century and which was inspired by Plato's *Timaeus*, the only work of Plato that was available in Latin until the twelfth century, by Boethius' *Consolation* and other works of ancient Latin Neoplatonism, by the theological works attributed to Dionysius the Areopagite, the disciple of St. Paul, but above all by the writings of St. Augustine. Augustine was perhaps the most vigorous philosophical thinker of Roman antiquity, and his thought was deeply affected by Platonic and Neoplatonic conceptions, much more than some of his recent interpreters are willing to admit. During the thirteenth century, Aristotelianism became the dominant philosophical current in the West, but the Platonic trend also received some impetus through new translations of Proclus and of certain Arabic writers; Augustinianism persisted as a strong secondary current, especially among the theologians of the Franciscan order; and even in the thought of such leading Aristotelians as Albert and Thomas, there is a recognizable strand of Augustinian and Neoplatonic conceptions.[4] During the fourteenth century, this Neoplatonic element assumes new strength in the speculative mysticism of Eckhart and his school, and the effect of these ideas was felt for several centuries, not only in Germany and the Low Countries, but also in Italy.

A second impulse of a very different nature came from the humanist movement of the early Italian Renaissance, which started as a literary and scholarly movement deeply concerned with the study and imitation of classical antiquity. There was a general curiosity about those ancient Greek writers and thinkers who had not been known to the Western Middle Ages, and a strong inclination to oppose Plato, who had been highly praised by Cicero and Augustine, to Aristotle, the chief authority of the scholastic philosophers. This tendency was expressed by Petrarch, who in his *Trionfo della Fama* introduces Plato first among the philosophers and assigns to Aristotle but the second place,[5] and who in one of his Latin treatises remarks dryly that Plato is praised by the greater authors, Aristotle by the greater number of people.[6] When the knowledge of Greek began to spread among Italian scholars after 1400, and a swelling stream of new translations began to increase the available heritage of ancient Greek literature and philosophy, some of Plato's most important works, such as the *Republic* and the *Laws*, the *Apology*, *Gorgias*, and *Phaedrus*, became known for the first time to Western readers, and rather widely known,[7] and the same was true for a few other Platonist and Neoplatonist writings. Yet the interest of the early Italian humanists in Plato and the Platonists was literary and eclectic, and there was no attempt to restate or rethink the ethical and metaphysical views of Plato and of his ancient successors. Consequently, we must admit that Renaissance Platonism was in many ways indebted to the humanistic movement, but we cannot agree that it was merely a part or aspect of that movement.

A third important impulse towards Renaissance Platonism came from the Byzantine East. Byzantine scholars throughout the Middle Ages had given much attention to ancient Greek philosophy, and especially to Plato and Neoplatonism. The most important figure in this tradition was Michael Psellus in the eleventh century whose work was still known to Renaissance scholars. During the very last decades of the Byzantine Empire, Neoplatonism was consciously revived in an attempt towards political and religious reform by a remarkable scholar and thinker, Georgius Gemistus Pletho.[8] He had enthusiastic disciples and also bitter enemies among his Byzantine contemporaries, and his work provided the starting point for a violent controversy between Platonists and Aristotelians that was continued for many decades in Italy by Byzantine exiles and by their Western pupils.[9] Pletho himself visited Italy in 1438 and apparently made a strong impression on those who met him, and the diffusion and influence of the writings of these Byzantine Platonists are becoming more and more evident. There are indeed good reasons for considering this Byzantine movement as the most immediate precedent of Renaissance Platonism, if not as its first major phase.

If we want to do justice to the Platonistic movement of the Western Renaissance, we must make allowance not only for its indebtedness to medieval, humanist, and Byzantine sources, but also for its direct acquaintance with Plato, Plotinus, Augustine, and other ancient Platonists, and also for a certain amount of original speculation. As the earliest representative of Renaissance Platonism we may consider Nicolaus Cusanus, who certainly was the most powerful thinker of the fifteenth century.[10] His contribution cannot be adequately described by labeling him a Platonist, yet his affinity with the Platonist current is undeniable, and his work exercised a persistent though sometimes intangible influence throughout the sixteenth century down to Giordano Bruno, who quotes him with the greatest admiration. The most conspicuous center of a revived Platonic philosophy was the Platonic Academy of Florence, which was active under the patronage of the Medici from 1462 to 1494 and had for its intellectual leader Marsilio Ficino, an inspiring teacher and writer who exercised a tremendous influence all over Europe through his translations and interpretations of Plato, of Plotinus, and of other Greek Neoplatonists as well as through his original philosophical works in which he professed to restate Platonist doctrine in basic agreement with Christian theology.[11] His work was supplemented in a quite independent manner by his younger friend, Giovanni Pico della Mirandola.[12] During the sixteenth century, Platonism as revived by the Byzantines, by Cusanus, and by the Florentine Academy became a broad and pervasive movement.[13] It derived its strength not so much from institutional support as from the diffusion of certain texts and ideas, and it found its followers among poets and writers, artists and theologians, as much as, or even more than, among the professional philosophers. In spite of these limitations, Platonism adds an important and unmistakable element to the theological controversies, the humanist rhetoric and scholarship, the Aristotelian logic and science, and the other intellectual pursuits of the period, and this element should not be overlooked. In Italy, Platonic philosophy was taught for some time at the universities of Pisa and Ferrara, and a few leading philosophers such as Patrizi and Bruno professedly or in fact followed a Platonist way of thinking. More than at the universities, Platonic philosophy, and especially its so-called philosophy of love, was cultivated at many academies during the sixteenth century—a new type of institution, half learned society and half literary club, which supplemented in many ways the intellectual activities of the older schools. The large body of love poetry and love literature that was written during the sixteenth century and in which certain ideas of Plato and of his recent disciples occupied an important place was at least in part connected with these academies. Besides many authors now forgotten, we find among the poets of this tradition Lorenzo de' Medici, Benivieni, and Michelangelo and among the prose writers Bembo, Castiglione, Leone Ebreo, and Tasso. We should have to give a long list of names if we wanted to mention the theologians and scientists or the writers on the arts and on music who were more or less profoundly influenced by the Platonist current. The movement was by no means limited to Italy. It had its followers in Spain[14] and in the Low Countries, and there are good reasons for counting among them no less a figure than Erasmus.[15] Platonism was strong in Germany and especially in France where it included many prominent scholars in Paris and in Lyons, and several poets, especially in the circle around Queen Marguerite of Navarre and in the Pléiade.[16] For England it is sufficient to mention John Colet, whose links with the Florentine Academy have recently been established beyond any doubt,[17] and the poet Spenser; it was there and especially at Cambridge that Renaissance Platonism found its most important sequel during the seventeenth century.[18]

When we try to sum up some of the major contributions, attitudes, and ideas of Renaissance Platonism, we should again keep in mind the variety and complexity of the movement. None of the ideas which we should like to consider as characteristic or significant was held by all or even a majority of Renaissance Platonists, and some of the most diffused ideas of Renaissance Platonism were not even derived from the earlier Platonic tradition, let alone from Plato himself.

The most obvious achievement of the Renaissance Platonists was in a sense the application of humanist scholarship to the ancient sources of Platonism, an activity which culminated in the work of Marsilio Ficino. Whereas the Western Middle Ages had possessed only a few works of Plato in translation, especially the *Timaeus* and the *Phaedo*, and a few works of Proclus,[19] the Renaissance obtained for the first time direct access to the entire work of Plato, of Plotinus, and of the other Platonist philosophers of Greek antiquity. This was in itself a major event in the intellectual history of Europe, and its importance was not diminished by the fact that the understanding of these Platonist sources continued to be affected by Neoplatonic and medieval ideas. For aside from their intrinsic merit and importance, these ancient Platonic writings supplied the West for the first time, through their sheer bulk, if you wish, with a substantial alternative to the philosophical doctrines taught by Aristotle and his commentators. This material was diffused along with the commentaries of the Renaissance Platonists and with their restatements of Platonist philosophy such as Ficino's *Platonic Theology*, works which made the writings of Plato more understandable and acceptable to contemporary readers, and which at the same time acquired for certain favorite ideas of their authors the venerable authority of Plato and of his ancient school. Renaissance Platonism thus became not only in the eyes of its representatives a Renaissance of Platonic philosophy,[20] but it also represents for the historian one of the most important phases and layers in the history of Platonism, a layer which the student of Plato will be careful to remove, whereas the historian of Platonism will give it his equally careful attention.

If we want to understand the impact of Renaissance Platonism upon the thought of the period, we must consider the way in which its representatives tried to combine Platonist ideas with the inherited traditions of Christian theology and of Aristotelian philosophy. Whereas the Byzantine Pletho had given an allegorical interpretation of ancient pagan mythology and had spoken in his writings so little of Christian theology that he could be accused of advocating a revival of ancient paganism, the Western Platonists of the Renaissance were convinced Christians who were more or less well versed in theology. They emphasized that Platonism and Christian theology based on reason were in basic agreement on several major points, and they made the most of Augustine's repeated remarks that the Platonists were closest among all ancient philosophers to the teachings of Christianity.[21] There is every reason to believe that the Renaissance Platonists were quite sincere in this conviction, and, at the same time, the proclaimed harmony between Platonism and Christianity goes a long way to explain the favor or tolerance which Platonism found with theologians and with the public at large, since the Renaissance was, modern assertions to the contrary notwithstanding, a basically religious age.

Less uniform was the attitude of the Renaissance Platonists towards the Aristotelian philosophy which continued to dominate in the schools and universities of the period. Pletho and several of his Byzantine and Italian followers had been hostile to the school of Aristotle, and the same attitude reappears during the later Renaissance in Patrizi and in several other philosophers and scientists. Yet even some of the followers of Pletho were more tolerant of Aristotle, and among the Florentine Platonists a different attitude prevailed. Ficino opposed Averroës and some of the Aristotelians of his own time on specific issues such as the unity of the intellect and the immortality of the soul, but his thought showed unmistakable traces of an Aristotelian training: he knew that the ancient Neoplatonists had intended to harmonize Plato and Aristotle, and he also felt that Aristotelian logic and natural philosophy, if not Aristotelian metaphysics, were needed as a supplement to Platonist philosophy. Pico della Mirandola went even farther: he undertook to prove the agreement between Plato and Aristotle; and in an interesting discussion with Ermolao Barbaro, a humanist Aristotelian, Pico the Renaissance Platonist assumed the defense of the medieval Arabic and Latin Aristotelians, a discussion that was resumed after Pico's death and in favor of Ermolao by a Protestant reformer sympathetic to Aristotle, Philipp Melanchthon.[22] This is one of the many curious instances from which we should learn that the actual lines of thought in the past history of philosophy were not drawn as we might expect if we merely go by labels or easy conventional generalizations.

Thus there was within Renaissance Platonism a strong tendency towards combining Platonist doctrine with Christian theology and with Aristotelian philosophy, and some of the most influential representatives of the movement advocated an even wider synthesis. Among the writings transmitted from Greek antiquity there was a body of works that showed certain similarities with Platonism and that was attributed to such venerable old authorities as Zoroaster, Hermes Trismegistus, Orpheus, and Pythagoras. Modern scholarship has shown that these writings were composed during the early centuries of our era, but the ancient Neoplatonists and Byzantine thinkers such as Psellus and Pletho accepted these writings as authentic witnesses of a pagan theology that was much older than Plato and should be considered as a source and confirmation of his philosophy. This tradition was enthusiastically received by Ficino, who translated some of these writings, and by most other Renaissance Platonists down to Patrizi, and they further enhanced the authority of these reputedly early texts by asserting that this ancient pagan theology, just as the Platonic philosophy which continued it, was in fundamental agreement with the theology of the Hebrews and Christians, a view for which again a number of Church Fathers could be cited as authorities.[23] This historical perspective was further broadened by Pico della Mirandola, who through his study of Hebrew became acquainted with the Jewish Cabala, which also purported to be of ancient origin, sensed its affinity with Platonist thought, and asserted its basic accordance with Christian theology, thus initiating an important current of Christian Cabalism which remained associated with Renaissance Platonism and affected many thinkers and writers of the sixteenth century.[24]

Behind these combinations of diverse sources, which to us must appear uncritical and unhistorical and which constitute what has been called the syncretism of the Renaissance Platonists, we may perceive a more fundamental conviction destined to exercise a profound influence upon the following centuries. For Ficino, the human intellect and will are naturally directed towards God, who is the sum total and ultimate source of truth and goodness. Consequently, philosophy as well as religion are natural to all men, and every historical form of religion or of philosophy will have some element of truth, though the degree of this truth will differ and some specific doctrines, such as Platonist philosophy and Christian theology, will attain to the highest degree.[25] It was in this spirit that Pico della Mirandola could propose to defend as true nine hundred theses taken from the most diverse ancient, Arabic, Jewish, and Christian thinkers.[26] This view makes it possible to recognize the partial merit and truth in other religions and philosophies and a common element in all, without being skeptical of one's own. In an age of passionate and often violent religious dispute such as the sixteenth and seventeenth centuries, the syncretism of the Platonists was clearly a source of inspiration for the advocates of peaceful discussion, of moderation and tolerance, from Erasmus to Bodin; at a later stage, it inspired the theories of natural religion, of deism, and of pantheism; and it was no coincidence that during the religious controversies of seventeenth century England, the moderate, latitudinarian position in theology found some of its chief supporters among the Cambridge Platonists.[27]

If we pass from the historical orientation of the Renaissance Platonists to some of their more specific philosophical ideas, we must first consider their theory of knowledge. One of the central points of Plato's philosophy was the theory of Ideas, according to which the pure forms or essences in which sense objects could merely participate constituted the only realm of true being and the only object of perfect and reliable knowledge. Platonists of later antiquity reinterpreted the Ideas as thoughts of the divine mind, and in this form the doctrine became an integral part of medieval theology and metaphysics. On the other hand, ancient Platonists down to Augustine insisted that the human soul possessed from birth certain basic concepts and principles related to the divine Ideas that were intrinsically true, that the mathematical disciplines provided an example of a body of valid knowledge derived from a priori principles independent of any sense perception, and that there was an active, a priori element even in sense perception. This doctrine had been largely abandoned by the Aristotelian philosophers of the later Middle Ages, who tended in their theory of knowledge towards a consistent empiricist position and derived all but formal logical thought through processes of abstraction from the data of sense perception. Renaissance Platonists such as Cusanus and Ficino brought the notion of innate ideas and principles back into prominence and thus paved the way for the later rationalistic position adopted by such thinkers as Descartes, Malebranche, Leibniz, and Kant. More specifically, the emphasis on the a priori certainty and perfection of mathematical knowledge, though not stressed in Florentine Platonism, was prominent in Cusanus, Patrizi, and other Platonists of the period, and though it was sometimes combined with the Pythagorean fancy for number symbolism, it was enthusiastically received by many mathematicians, as well as by theorists of music and of the visual arts, and it had a definite impact upon early modern physical science, as can be seen in the case of Galileo and especially of Kepler.[28] For the new effort to understand the physical universe in terms of strict mathematical laws found a more congenial background in the Platonists' emphasis on mathematical certainty than in the Aristotelian cosmology which was based on substances and their qualities and on a rigid separation between the celestial and elementary spheres.

This emphasis on mathematics that seems to prepare the way for the mathematical physics of modern times was combined in the cosmology of the Renaissance Platonists with a very different set of ideas, which to the modern observer must appear as the very opposite of a scientific conception of the physical universe. Aristotelian cosmology did not give sufficient prominence to mathematical relations, to be sure, but it was essentially a sober system in which the qualities and operations of physical substances could be discussed in terms of empirical observation and of logical inference. Yet Renaissance Platonists such as Ficino were not satisfied to consider the universe as a hierarchy of substances, as their medieval predecessors had done, but for them the world possessed a kind of inner life and unity that held it together and connected every part of it with all the others.[29] Thus the Neoplatonic notion of the world soul acquired a new importance, and the existing substances such as stars, elements, minerals, plants, and animals were thought to be full of different powers, affinities, and antipathies which man was capable of knowing and even of manipulating to his advantage. These notions were taken up by many natural philosophers of the sixteenth and early seventeenth centuries down to Campanella, and they were more often than not combined with the occult sciences of astrology, alchemy, and magic, which had been taken over from the Arabs during the high Middle Ages and which acquired during the Renaissance, partly in alliance with Platonism, a greater importance and diffusion than ever before. The subject is rather complex and difficult to judge from this distance. The interest and the belief in the occult sciences were not limited to Platonists or shared by all of them. Moreover, they were not incompatible with genuine scientific interests, as has been shown so convincingly by recent studies in the history of science.[30] Many scientists believed in astrology or alchemy, and, on the other hand, many opponents of the occult sciences were motivated by religious rather than by scientific considerations. It also was possible to accept astrology but to oppose alchemy, or to reject judiciary astrology but to approve the general principle that the stars exert occult influences upon earthly events. The lines between the genuine and the pseudo sciences were not drawn as clearly or in the same manner as they are now. The Renaissance was, whether we like it or not, a superstitious and fantastic age, and description of its thought, and especially of Renaissance Platonism, that failed to mention this aspect would be quite one-sided and incomplete. When I say that it was possible to be respectable and superstitious at the same time, I intend to excuse the Renaissance, not to praise it. Nor do I feel any satisfaction when I must state that it has been equally possible in more recent times, and even in our times, to be respectable and superstitious, though the forms of superstition have somewhat changed. We are all capable of seeing the truth on some matters and of missing it on others, and hence it is our task, not to condemn or glorify, but to criticize each other. The historian finds himself in a somewhat similar position when he ventures to judge the past.

Having discussed the cosmology of Renaissance Platonism, we are better able to understand the place which it assigns to man in the universe.[31] Renaissance humanists tended to attach particular importance to man and to his dignity, and to base on this notion the claims they made for the moral value of their literary and scholarly studies, the "humanities." The Platonists were not only affected by this idea, but they were also able to put it into a far more significant cosmological and metaphysical framework. They inherited from ancient and medieval speculation the concept of man as a microcosm, a smaller world which participates in all the properties and powers of the whole universe. They also inherited the idea that man and his soul are placed, as it were, on the borderline between the intelligible or eternal and the visible or mortal realms. Yet they gave a novel and in a sense original interpretation to those concepts. In Cusanus, Christ as God and man mediates between God and the whole universe since human nature participates in that of all other created things.[32] In Ficino, the Neoplatonic hierarchy of substances that descends from God to matter is consciously reshuffled in order to assign the central place in the hierarchy to the human soul, which thus mediates between the upper and the lower half of the universe.[33] In several eloquent passages he praises man for his universality since in his thought, his desires, and his actions he encompasses the whole universe and strives to ascend towards God as far as this is possible for him. Pico, both in his famous oration and in his other writings, goes one step farther in his praise of man's dignity: man no longer occupies a fixed place in the hierarchy of things, not even in its center, but he freely moves upwards and downwards, possesses no definite nature of his own, and determines his condition by his own moral and intellectual choice.[34] On the other hand, man is exalted as the born ruler of nature, a view that was to receive new meaning in Francis Bacon, and to exercise through him a powerful influence on the course of modern thought.

Yet unlike Bacon and his modern followers, the Renaissance Platonists were no activists. Their ideal was that of the contemplative life, and their moral thought was dominated by the spiritual experience of an inner ascent which leads the soul through several degrees of knowledge and of love to the immediate vision and enjoyment of God.[35] The entire meaning of human life is understood with reference to this ultimate experience, and in so far as the final vision of God seems to be attainable in this life, at least for a few persons and for a short while, the Renaissance Platonists reveal themselves as the successors not only of the ancient Neoplatonists but also of the medieval mystics and spirituals. The broad and deep appeal which Florentine Platonism had both among its contemporaries and during the sixteenth century seems to originate to a large extent in this central feature of its thought. Renaissance Platonism was able to express the deepest mystical experiences and aspirations of an age that was both Christian and classical in its temper.

The emphasis on man and on his central place in the universe and the tendency to find the basic meaning of human life in the inner ascent towards God go a long way to explain the preoccupation of Renaissance Platonism, and of Renaissance thought in general, with the immortality of the soul.[36] Plato had formulated several arguments for immortality in his *Phaedo*, and the immortality of the soul had been accepted ever since in the philosophical tradition of Platonism and later in Christian theology. Aristotle did not express himself very clearly on individual immortality, and hence the Aristotelian philosophers of the later Middle Ages and of the Renaissance were divided on the question of whether the immortality of the soul could be demonstrated on purely rational or Aristotelian grounds. For the Renaissance Platonists the question was of paramount importance, and it is not surprising that Ficino dedicated to it his major philosophical work, the *Platonic Theology*. The exalted position of man and of his soul in the universe seemed to demand its immortality, and the very ascent of the soul towards the contemplation of God, which constitutes its chief task, can be accomplished during the present life by but few persons and for a short while. If the fundamental end of human existence is to be justified, a future life and the immortality of the soul must be postulated in order to make this ultimate end attainable for many persons and forever. Thus the intimate aspirations felt by many thoughtful persons received metaphysical justification, and Ficino's arguments for immortality were eagerly repeated by many poets and theologians and even by some Aristotelian philosophers. It seems significant for the preoccupations of the period as well as for the influence of Platonist thought that it was exactly in 1513 at the Lateran Council when the immortality of the soul was for the first time officially proclaimed as a dogma of the Catholic Church, after it had been generally accepted or presupposed as a matter of course for so many centuries.

Let us finally consider some of the contributions of Renaissance Platonism to the political and social thought of the period. Plato had dedicated his two largest works, the *Republic* and the *Laws*, to a discussion of the perfect society, but this political element, though important within the context of Plato's own life and time, was neglected by most of his ancient and medieval followers. In the Renaissance also, most Platonists did not emphasize the political aspects of Plato's thought. Yet Thomas More's *Utopia*, different as it is in its aim and content from Plato's *Republic*, could not have been written without the Platonic model, and from More derives a long line of political Utopias that leads through Campanella's *City of the Sun* to the eighteenth and early nineteenth centuries. Political utopianism had one of its chief sources in Plato, and although the leading Platonists of the Renaissance were not concerned with this aspect of Plato's thought, they still were instrumental in making his *Republic* and *Laws* available to Western thinkers.

In its prevailing outlook, Renaissance Platonism was individualistic rather than political, and it has even been criticized by modern historians for this very reason. Still it was not as exclusively concerned with the solitary life of the individual person as is

often believed. Renaissance Platonists show a feeling for the soli-
darity of all mankind that is reminiscent of the Stoics and of
Cicero and that is occasionally expressed in moving and eloquent
passages.[37] This view is not elaborated or prominently stated,
but it is clearly consistent with the central ideas and convictions
of the school. More influential and also better known is the
theory of human love and friendship developed by the Platonists.[38] This theory drew upon a number of diverse sources:
Plato's doctrine of love as expressed in the *Symposium* and *Phaedrus*
and as interpreted by Plotinus and other ancient Platonists; the
Christian concept of neighborly love (*charitas*) as it had been
developed by Paul and Augustine; ancient theories of friendship
formulated by Aristotle, by the Stoics, and especially by the
Epicureans; finally, courtly love as it appears transformed in the
early Italian poets down to Dante and Petrarch. When Ficino
formulated his theory of Platonic love in his commentary on
Plato's *Symposium* and in some other writings (and the curious
term was actually coined by him), he drew upon all these earlier
doctrines, but gave the theory a somewhat novel meaning which
was closely connected with his own philosophical principles.
Love and friendship in the Platonic sense are for him the relationship between two or more persons who all participate in the contemplative life. Their relation to each other, as Ficino puts it, is
based on the relation each of them has to God, and for this reason
it is also called divine love. It is this divine love which constitutes
the spiritual bond that united master and pupils in the Florentine
Academy. During the sixteenth century this notion of love exercised as wide an influence as any other theory associated with
Renaissance Platonism. Poets and popular writers had spoken for
a long time of love and its power, but now the Platonist theory
supplied a novel justification or pretext for a serious and detailed
treatment of the favorite subject, and, besides Ficino himself,
such important thinkers as Pico, Diacceto, Leone Ebreo, Patrizi,
and Bruno took part in the discussion. The vogue is probably
best understood if we say that Platonist philosophers considered

the theory and philosophy of love as the most appropriate way for expressing the conception of human relationship in a manner that was connected and consistent with their general metaphysical principles, and that less serious writers used the Platonic theory to add an air of apparent importance to their otherwise frivolous reasonings on the subject. Platonic love has long ceased to be fashionable, and nobody has written love treatises for some time. Yet if we remember that Spinoza probably borrowed his central term, the intellectual love of God, from the Renaissance Platonists, and that these affected the thought of such poets as Michelangelo, Tasso, Spenser, and Du Bellay, their love speculation will not appear to have been completely ephemeral.[39]

In our brief survey of Renaissance Platonism, we have mentioned only a few of its ideas which seemed to be especially significant or influential, and many more might be added, such as the notion of the divine madness of the poet which was derived from Plato's *Phaedrus* and *Ion* and began to spread during the sixteenth century.[40] The influence of Renaissance Platonism upon the following centuries was as varied as were its ideas, and we have mentioned already some major instances. Platonist cosmology was in many ways associated with the belief in the occult dynamics of nature that was gradually abandoned in the natural sciences during the seventeenth and eighteenth centuries, but survived in various forms of modern occultism and theosophy, and also in the tradition of romantic poetry. (Poets are apt to feel nostalgia for the distant and the past: in a scientific age, they cling to the occult forces of nature, as in many Christian centuries they were enchanted with classical mythology.) The syncretism of the Platonists and their respect for the truth contained in the thought of many diverse philosophies and religions prepared the way for deism, the most important alternative to the religious orthodoxies and to radical atheism. The stress on innate ideas and a priori knowledge, and especially on the absolute certainty of mathematics, was an important contribution which survived in the rationalistic and idealistic aspects of modern science and philosophy with Kepler and Galileo, Descartes and Leibniz, aspects that have been sometimes exaggerated or radically opposed, but that are still alive in contemporary scientific and philosophical thought. Finally, the very revival of Platonism and the diffusion of the text of Plato and Plotinus transmitted to the subsequent centuries the prestige and content of Platonic philosophy and made it possible for later generations up to the present to be differently inspired by these sources. Renaissance Platonism was not merely an echo of medieval Platonism or an episode within Renaissance humanism but an important and partly original philosophical movement. It represents one of the major phases in the history of Platonism, and as such it made a powerful contribution to the thought and literature of the sixteenth century and to the subsequent development of superstition, of science, and of philosophy down to the present day.

NOTES

1. J. Burckhardt, *Die Cultur der Renaissance in Italien* (Basel, 1860).

2. E. Cassirer, *Das Erkenntnisproblem*, Vol. I (Berlin, 1922), *Individuum und Kosmos in der Philosophie der Renaissance* (Berlin-Leipzig, 1927); E. Cassirer, P. O. Kristeller, and J. H. Randall, Jr. (eds), *The Renaissance Philosophy of Man* (Chicago, 1948); F. Ueberweg, *Grundriss der Geschichte der Philosophie*, Vol. III (12th ed., Berlin, 1924); E. Garin, *La Filosofia*, 2 vols. (Milan, 1947); G. Saitta, *Il pensiero italiano nell' umanesimo e nel rinascimento*, 3 vols. (Bologna, 1949-51); P. O. Kristeller and J. H. Randall, Jr., "The Study of the Renaissance," *Journal of the History of Ideas*, II (1941), 449-496; P. O. Kristeller, *The Classics and Renaissance Thought* (Cambridge, Mass., 1955), *Studies in Renaissance Thought and Letters* (Rome, 1956); G. de Santillana, *The Age of Adventure* (New York, 1956).

3. N. A. Robb, *Neoplatonism of the Italian Renaissance* (London, 1935); R. Klibansky, *The Continuity of the Platonic Tradition during the Middle Ages* (London, 1939 and 1950); Kristeller, *Classics*, pp. 48 ff.

4. C. Fabro, *La Nozione metafisica di participazione secondo S. Tommaso d'Aquino* (Milan, 1939; 2nd ed., Turin, 1950); L. B. Geiger, *La participation dans la philosophie de S. Thomas d'Aquin* (Paris, 1942); A. Little, *The Platonic Heritage of Thomism* (Dublin, 1949).

5. III, 4-7.

6. Petrarca, *La Traité "De sui ipsius et multorum ignorantia,"* ed. L. M. Capelli (Paris, 1906), pp. 72-73.

7. E. Garin, "Ricerche sulle traduzioni di Platone nalla prima metà del sec. XV," in *Medioevo e Rinascimento: Studi in onore di Bruno Nardi* (Florence, 1955), I, 339-374. Plato's *Lysis* was also translated by Pier Candido Decembrio.

8. M. V. Anastos, "Pletho's Calendar and Liturgy," *Dumbarton Oaks Papers*, IV (1948), 183-305; F. Masai, *Plethon et le Platonisme de Mistra* (Paris, 1956).

9. L. Mohler, *Aus Bessarions Gelehrtenkreis* (Paderborn, 1942).

10. E. Vansteenberghe, *La cardinal Nicolas de Cues* (Paris, 1920). Many of Cusanus' writings, and several monographic studies concerning him, have been recently published by the Heidelberg Academy.

11. A. Della Torre, *Storia dell' Accademia Platonica di Firenze* (Florence, 1902); G. Saitta, *Marsilio Ficino e la filosofia dell' umanesimo* (3rd ed., Bologna, 1954); Kristeller, *The Philosophy of Marsilio Ficino* (New York, 1943) [*Il pensiero filosofico di Marsilio Ficino* (Florence, 1953)], *Studies in Renaissance Thought and Letters* (Rome, 1956); A. Chastel, *Marsile Ficin et l'Art* (Geneva, 1954); Marsile Ficin, *Commentaire sur le Banquet de Platon*, ed. R. Marcel (Paris, 1956).

12. Garin, *Giovanni Pico della Mirandola* (Florence, 1937); E. Anagnine, G. *Pico della Mirandola* (Bari, 1937); A. Dulles, *Princeps Concordiae* (Cambridge, Mass., 1941); Cassirer, "Giovanni Pico della Mirandola," *Journal of the History of Ideas*, III (1942), 123-144, 319-346.

13. Robb, *Neoplatonism;* Kristeller, *Studies*, pp. 287 ff.

14. U. Gonzalez de la Calle, *Sebastian Fox Morcillo* (Madrid, 1903).

15. This is especially apparent in the last chapters of his *Praise of Folly.*

16. W. Moench, *Die italienische Platonrenaissance und ihre Bedeutung für Frankreichs Literatur und Geistesgeschichte* (Berlin, 1936); J. Festugière, *La philosophie de l'amour de Marsile Ficin et son influence sur la littérature française au XVIe siècle* (Paris, 1941).

17. R. Marcel, "Les 'découvertes' d'Erasme en Angleterre," *Bibliothèque d'Humanisme et Renaissance*, XIV (1952), 117-123.

18. J. W. Bennett, "The Theme of Spenser's Fowre Hymnes," *Studies in Philology*, XXVIII (1931), 18-57; S. Jayne, "Ficino and the Platonism of the English Renaissance," *Comparative Literature*, IV (1952), 214-238.

19. *Corpus Platonicum Medii Aevi*, ed. R. Klibansky (London, 1940, *et seqq.*).

20. Kristeller, *The Philosophy*, pp. 22-23 (*Il pensiero*, p. 13).

21. Kristeller, *Studies*, pp. 368 and 13.

22. Q. Breen, "Giovanni Pico della Mirandola on the Conflict of Philosophy and Rhetoric," *Journal of the History of Ideas*, XIII (1952), 384-426.

23. Karl H. Dannenfeldt, "The Renaissance and Pre-Classical Civilization," *Journal of the History of Ideas*, XIII (1952), 435-449; D. P. Walker, "Orpheus the Theologian and Renaissance Platonists," *Journal of the Warburg and Courtauld Institutes*, XVI (1953), 100-120, "The Prisca Theologia in France," *Journal . . .,*XVII (1954), 204-259; Kristeller, *Studies*, pp. 221 ff.

24. J. Blau, *The Christian Interpretation of the Cabala in the Renaissance* (New York, 1944).

25. Kristeller, *The Philosophy*, p. 316 (*Il pensiero*, pp. 342 ff.).

26. Anagnine, G. *Pico della Mirandola* (see note 12 above).

27. Cassirer, *The Platonic Renaissance in England* (New York, 1953).

28. E. A. Burtt, *The Metaphysical Foundations of Modern Physical Science* (New York, 1951); Cassirer, "Galileo's Platonism," in *Studies and Essays in the History of Science and Learning in Honor of George Sarton* (New York, 1946), pp. 279-297.

29. Kristeller, *The Philosophy*, p. 92 (*Il pensiero*, pp. 86 ff.).

30. L. Thorndike, *A History of Magic and Experimental Science*, 6 vols. (New York, 1923-41).

31. G. Gentile, "Il concetto dell' uomo nel Rinascimento," in his *Il pensiero italiano del Rinascimento* (3rd ed., Florence, 1940), pp. 47-113; Kristeller, *Studies*, pp. 261 ff.

32. Nicolaus Cusanus, *De docta ignorantia*, III, ii-iv (*Of Learned Ignorance*, trans. G. Heron, London, 1954, p. 131).

33. Kristeller, *The Philosophy*, p. 106 (*Il pensiero*, p. 102).

34. *Ibid.*, in *The Renaissance Philosophy of Man*, pp. 215 ff.

35. Kristeller, *The Philosophy*, p. 223 (*Il pensiero*, p. 237).

36. *Ibid.*, *The Philosophy*, p. 324 (*Il pensiero*, p. 350).

37. *Ibid.*, *The Philosophy*, p. 113 (*Il pensiero*, p. 111), *Studies*, pp. 271 ff.

38. *Ibid.*, *The Philosophy*, p. 256 (*Il pensiero*, p. 274).

39. P. Lorenzetti, *La bellezza e l'amore nei trattati del Cinquecento* (Pisa, 1917); L. Tonelli, *L'amore nella poesia e nel pensiero del Rinascimento* (Florence, 1933).

40. E. Zilsel, *Die Entstehung des Geniebegriffes* (Tübingen, 1926), pp. 274 ff.

Biographical Notes

WALLACE K. FERGUSON was born in a Methodist parsonage a few miles north of Toronto, Ontario, in 1902. He received his A.B. in the Honors Course in English and History at the University of Western Ontario in 1924. A recipient of the President White Fellowship in History, he attended Cornell University, where he received the master's degree in 1925 and the doctor's degree in 1927. The year 1927-28 he spent in Europe on a Social Service Research Council Fellowship. Upon his return, he was appointed instructor in history at New York University, where he was advanced to assistant professor in 1930, to associate professor in 1940, and to professor in 1945. During 1939-40 he held a Guggenheim Fellowship. From 1945 to 1952 he was a member of the National Committee on Renaissance Studies of the American Council of Learned Societies and, later, was also a member of the committee which founded the Renaissance Society of America. In 1954 he was awarded an honorary doctor's degree by the University of Western Ontario. In 1956 he was appointed head of the history department at that university, and in 1958 he was made a fellow of the Royal Society of Canada.

Professor Ferguson is the author of the following books: *Erasmi Opuscula: A Supplement to the Opera Omnia*, The Hague, 1933; *A Survey of European Civilization*, Part I, Boston, 1936; Swedish translation, Stockholm, 1938; *The Renaissance*, New York, 1940; *The Renaissance in Historical Thought, Five Centuries of Interpretation*, Boston, 1948; French translation, Paris, 1950. He is also the author of a number of articles in learned journals.

MYRON P. GILMORE began his studies of history at Amherst College under the late Laurence Bradford Packard. In 1932, he received his A.B. degree *summa cum laude* and was awarded a fellowship for graduate study at Harvard. Two years later he was awarded a travelling fellowship for research and study in Europe. This made it possible for him to spend the academic year 1934-35 in France and Italy, where he became interested in the relationship between French and Italian thought in the age of the Renaissance. Upon his return from Europe he was appointed a teaching fellow in history at Harvard. After receiving his doctor's degree he was appointed to an instructorship at Harvard in 1938. From 1942 until 1946 he served in the United States Naval Reserve. In 1943 he was promoted to associate professor at Harvard. He became professor of history in 1953 and since 1955 has served as chairman of the department. In September 1955 he was a delegate to the International Congress of Historical Sciences in Rome and presided over the section on the Renaissance. During 1956-57 he studied in Rome on a Fulbright Award and a Guggenheim Memorial Foundation Fellowship.

Professor Gilmore is the author of the following books: *Argument from Roman Law in Political Thought, 1200-1600,* Harvard University Press, 1940; *The World of Humanism,* Harper, 1953; and *Erasmus, the Scholar and the World,* now in press. He is also the author of a number of articles in learned journals.

E. HARRIS HARBISON, born in Sewickley, Pennsylvania, in 1907, received his A.B. degree from Princeton in 1928, his master's degree in 1932 from Harvard, and his doctor's degree, also from Harvard, in 1938. For the academic year 1935-36, Harvard awarded him the Bayard Cutting Travelling Fellowship for studies in Europe. He has been a member of the faculty of Princeton University since 1933 and Henry Charles Lea Professor of History at Princeton since 1945. In 1957 he was M. D. Anderson Visiting Professor at Rice Institute. He has served on the editorial board of the *Journal of Modern History,* and is a member of the council of the Renaissance Society of America and of the American Society for Reformation Research. He has been a trustee of Princeton Theological Seminary since 1951.

Professor Harbison's first book, *Rival Ambassadors at the Court of Queen Mary 1553-57,* 1940, won the Herbert Baxter Adams prize of the American Historical Association. He is also the author of *The Age of Reformation,* 1955, and has contributed chapters to *Socialism and American Life,* 1952; *Great Problems in European Civilization,* 1954; *General Education in School and College,* 1952, and *The Christian Idea of Education,* 1957. His most recent book, *The Christian Scholar in the Age of the Reformation,* 1956, contains the lectures which he prepared for the Arensberg Lecture Series on the Renaissance at the University of Southern California. Professor Harbison is also the author of numerous articles dealing with the Christian conception of history.

PAUL OSKAR KRISTELLER was born in Berlin, Germany, on May 22, 1905. After graduating from the Mommsen-Gymnasium in Berlin-Charlottenburg in 1923, he studied at the universities of Berlin, Freiburg, Marburg, and Heidelberg, receiving the doctor's degree in philosophy from the University of Heidelberg in 1928. In 1931, he passed the State Examinations in Greek, Latin, and Philosophy, whereupon he did research at the University of Freiburg from 1931 to 1933. During 1932-33 he held a Fellowship of the Notgemeinschaft der Deutschen Wissenschaft. During 1934-35, he was lecturer in German at the Instituto Superiore di Magistero in Florence, Italy. From 1935 to 1938, he taught German literature at the Scuola Normale Superiore and the University of Pisa. He was appointed lecturer in philosophy at Yale University in 1939, served as associate in philosophy at Columbia University from 1939 to 1948, as associate professor from 1948 to 1956, and has since been professor of philosophy at Columbia. In 1949, he was a visiting professor at the Scuola Normale Superiore in Pisa. He returned to the same institution in 1952 as Fulbright Lecturer. In 1954, he gave the Martin Lectures at Oberlin College. He has served as book editor of the *Journal of Philosophy*, is a member of the editorial boards of the *Journal of the History of Ideas* and of *Manuscripta*. He is a Fellow of the American Academy of Arts and Sciences and a member of the executive board of the Renaissance Society of America. He serves as secretary for an international scholarly project, Medieval and Renaissance Latin Translations and Commentaries, and is codirector of Nuova Collezione di Testi Umanistici inediti o rari, published for the Scuola Normale Superiore of Pisa. During the academic year 1954-55, he was a member of the Institute for Advanced Study at Princeton. In 1958 he was awarded a Guggenheim Fellowship.

Professor Kristeller is the author of the following books: *Der Begriff der Seele in der Ethik des Plotin*, 1929; *The Philosophy of Marsilio Ficino*, Columbia University Press, 1943; Italian translation, 1953; *The Classics and Renaissance Thought*, Harvard University Press, 1955; *Studies in Renaissance Thought and Letters*, Rome, 1956. He is the editor of *Supplementum Ficinianum: Marsilii Ficini Florentini Opuscula inedita et dispersa*, 2 vols., Florence, 1937, and a co-editor of *The Renaissance Philosophy of Man*, University of Chicago Press, 1948. In addition, Professor Kristeller is the author of over fifty articles in learned journals.

GARRETT MATTINGLY was born in Washington, D.C., on May 6, 1900. During World War I he served with the 43rd United States Infantry. He then studied at Harvard, where he received his A.B. in 1923, his master's degree in 1926, and his Ph.D. in 1935. From 1922 to 1924, he studied abroad on a Sheldon Fellowship from Harvard University. He was an instructor at Northwestern University from 1926 to 1928, and taught at Long Island University from 1928 to 1942. He was awarded Guggenheim Fellowships for 1937-38, 1946, and 1953. During World War II he served in the United States Naval Reserve. From 1946 to 1948 he was chairman of the Cooper Union Forum and head of the Division of Social Philosophy at that institution. He was professor of European history at Columbia University from 1948 until his death in 1962.

Professor Mattingly was the author of *Catherine of Aragon: A Biography*, Boston, 1941; *Renaissance Diplomacy*, London and Boston, 1955. He was the editor of *A Further Supplement to the Calendar of State Papers, Spanish*, 1513-1543. In addition, he wrote numerous articles for learned journals, mostly about diplomatic history in the fifteenth and sixteenth centuries.

Index

hᴀʀᴘᴇʀ 🔥 ᴛᴏʀᴄʜʙᴏᴏᴋs

HUMANITIES AND SOCIAL SCIENCES

American Studies

Anthropology & Sociology

Art and Art History

Business, Economics & Economic History

NORMAN COHN: The Pursuit of the Millennium: *Revolutionary Messianism in medieval and Reformation Europe and its bearing on modern totalitarian movements* TB/1037

ARTHUR O. LOVEJOY: The Great Chain of Being: *A Study of the History of an Idea* TB/1009

ROBERT PAYNE: Hubris: *A Study of Pride.* Foreword by Sir Herbert Read TB/1031

BRUNO SNELL: The Discovery of the Mind: *The Greek Origins of European Thought* TB/1018

PAUL VALÉRY: The Outlook for Intelligence TB/2016

Literature, Poetry, The Novel & Criticism

JAMES BAIRD: Ishmael: *The Art of Melville in the Contexts of International Primitivism* TB/1023

JACQUES BARZUN: The House of Intellect TB/1051

W. J. BATE: From Classic to Romantic: *Premises of Taste in Eighteenth Century England* TB/1036

RACHEL BESPALOFF: On the Iliad TB/2006

R. P. BLACKMUR, et al.: Lectures in Criticism. *Introduction by Huntington Cairns* TB/2003

ABRAHAM CAHAN: The Rise of David Levinsky: *a novel. Introduction by John Higham* TB/1028

ERNST R. CURTIUS: European Literature and the Latin Middle Ages TB/2015

GEORGE ELIOT: Daniel Deronda: *a novel. Introduction by F. R. Leavis* TB/1039

ETIENNE GILSON: Dante and Philosophy TB/1089

ALFRED HARBAGE: As They Liked It: *A Study of Shakespeare's Moral Artistry* TB/1035

STANLEY R. HOPPER, Ed.: Spiritual Problems in Contemporary Literature TB/21

A. R. HUMPHREYS: The Augustan World: *Society, Thought, and Letters in Eighteenth Century England* TB/1105

HENRY JAMES: The Princess Casamassima: *a novel. Introduction by Clinton F. Oliver* TB/1005

HENRY JAMES: Roderick Hudson: *a novel. Introduction by Leon Edel* TB/1016

HENRY JAMES: The Tragic Muse: *a novel. Introduction by Leon Edel* TB/1017

ARNOLD KETTLE: An Introduction to the English Novel. Volume I: *Defoe to George Eliot* TB/1011
Volume II: *Henry James to the Present* TB/1012

JOHN STUART MILL: On Bentham and Coleridge. *Introduction by F. R. Leavis* TB/1070

PERRY MILLER & T. H. JOHNSON, Editors: The Puritans: *A Sourcebook of Their Writings*
Volume I TB/1093
Volume II TB/1094

KENNETH B. MURDOCK: Literature and Theology in Colonial New England TB/99

SAMUEL PEPYS: The Diary of Samuel Pepys. *Edited by O. F. Morshead. Illustrations by Ernest Shepard* TB/1007

ST.-JOHN PERSE: Seamarks TB/2002

GEORGE SANTAYANA: Interpretations of Poetry and Religion TB/9

C. P. SNOW: Time of Hope: *a novel* TB/1040

DOROTHY VAN GHENT: The English Novel: *Form and Function* TB/1050

MORTON DAUWEN ZABEL, Editor: Literary Opinion in America
Volume I TB/3013
Volume II TB/3014

Myth, Symbol & Folklore

JOSEPH CAMPBELL, Editor: Pagan and Christian Mysteries TB/2013

MIRCEA ELIADE: Cosmos and History: *The Myth of the Eternal Return* TB/50

C. G. JUNG & C. KERÉNYI: Essays on a Science of Mythology: *The Myths of the Divine Child and the Divine Maiden* TB/2014

ERWIN PANOFSKY: Studies in Iconology: *Humanistic Themes in the Art of the Renaissance. 180 illustrations* TB/1077

JEAN SEZNEC: The Survival of the Pagan Gods: *The Mythological Tradition and its Place in Renaissance Humanism and Art. 108 illustrations* TB/2004

HEINRICH ZIMMER: Myths and Symbols in Indian Art and Civilization. *70 illustrations* TB/2005

Philosophy

HENRI BERGSON: Time and Free Will: *An Essay on the Immediate Data of Consciousness* TB/1021

H. J. BLACKHAM: Six Existentialist Thinkers: *Kierkegaard, Nietzsche, Jaspers, Marcel, Heidegger, Sartre* TB/1002

ERNST CASSIRER: Rousseau, Kant and Goethe. *Introduction by Peter Gay* TB/1092

FREDERICK COPLESTON: Medieval Philosophy TB/76

F. M. CORNFORD: From Religion to Philosophy: *A Study in the Origins of Western Speculation* TB/20

WILFRID DESAN: The Tragic Finale: *An Essay on the Philosophy of Jean-Paul Sartre* TB/1030

ETIENNE GILSON: Dante and Philosophy TB/1089

WILLIAM CHASE GREENE: Moira: *Fate, Good, and Evil in Greek Thought* TB/1104

W. K. C. GUTHRIE: The Greek Philosophers: *From Thales to Aristotle* TB/1008

F. H. HEINEMANN: Existentialism and the Modern Predicament TB/28

IMMANUEL KANT: Lectures on Ethics. *Introduction by Lewis W. Beck* TB/105

WILLARD VAN ORMAN QUINE: From a Logical Point of View: *Logico-Philosophical Essays* TB/566

BERTRAND RUSSELL et al.: The Philosophy of Bertrand Russell. *Edited by Paul Arthur Schilpp*
Volume I TB/1095
Volume II TB/1096

L. S. STEBBING: A Modern Introduction to Logic TB/538

ALFRED NORTH WHITEHEAD: Process and Reality: *An Essay in Cosmology* TB/1033

WILHELM WINDELBAND: A History of Philosophy I: *Greek, Roman, Medieval* TB/38

WILHELM WINDELBAND: A History of Philosophy II: *Renaissance, Enlightenment, Modern* TB/39

Philosophy of History

NICOLAS BERDYAEV: The Beginning and the End TB/14

NICOLAS BERDYAEV: The Destiny of Man TB/61

WILHELM DILTHEY: Pattern and Meaning in History: *Thoughts on History and Society. Edited with an Introduction by H. P. Rickman* TB/1075

JOSE ORTEGA Y GASSET: The Modern Theme. *Introduction by Jose Ferrater Mora* TB/1038

W. H. WALSH: Philosophy of History: *An Introduction* TB/1020

Political Science & Government

JEREMY BENTHAM: The Handbook of Political Fallacies. *Introduction by Crane Brinton* TB/1069

Psychology

RELIGION

Ancient & Classical

Biblical Thought & Literature

Christianity: Origins & Early Development

Christianity: The Middle Ages and After

Judaic Thought & Literature

NATURAL SCIENCES AND MATHEMATICS

Biological Sciences